WHEN SEARCH MEETS WEB USABILITY

SHARI THUROW AND **NICK MUSICA**

New Riders

VOICES THAT MATTER™

When Search Meets Web Usability
Shari Thurow and Nick Musica

New Riders
1249 Eighth Street
Berkeley, CA 94710
510/524-2178
510/524-2221 (fax)

Find us on the web at www.newriders.com
To report errors, please send a note to errata@peachpit.com

New Riders is an imprint of Peachpit Press, a division of Pearson Education

Copyright © 2009 by Shari Thurow and Nick Musica

Project Editor: Nancy Peterson
Development Editor: Robyn G. Thomas
Technical Editors: Anne Kennedy and John Sorflaten
Production Coordinator: Myrna Vladic
Copy Editor: Doug Adrianson
Compositor: David Van Ness
Marketing Manager: Glenn Bisignani
Indexer: Valerie Perry
Cover and interior design: Mimi Heft
Cover photo: Francois Roux
Cover production: Mike Tanamachi

ISBN 13: 978-0-321-60589-4
ISBN 10:   0-321-60589-6

9 8 7 6 5 4 3 2 1

Printed and bound in the United States of America

Dedications

To our parents:
Dale and Edwin Thurow
Susan and Nicholas Musica

And in loving memory:
Big Jim Schultz
Donald Londrie
Jack Wendt
Tierney Smutny

■ ABOUT THE AUTHORS

Shari Thurow is the founder and Search Engine Optimization (SEO) Director for Omni Marketing Interactive, a full-service search engine optimization, web design, and website usability firm. As the leading expert on search-engine-friendly web design, Shari lectures on this topic and works for many firms worldwide.

She is also the author of *Search Engine Visibility* (New Riders, 2007), which teaches web developers how to build a site that pleases both site visitors and the commercial web search engines. *Search Engine Visibility* has been translated into French, Japanese, Korean, and Polish.

Clients include Microsoft, AOL, Yahoo, National Cancer Institute, HSBC, Expedia, WebMD and MedicineNet.com, ABC News, Wharton School of the University of Pennsylvania, and Dow Corning.

Additionally, Shari has designed and successfully marketed websites for businesses in fields such as medicine, science, biotechnology, accounting and finance, computers and software, manufacturing, real estate, law, e-commerce and online stores, art and design, marketing, insurance, employment, education, and travel.

Shari has been featured in many publications, including the *New York Times*, *USA Today*, *Wired Magazine*, *Entrepreneur*, *Internet Retailer*, and *Crain's Chicago Business*.

Shari received her B.A. in Genetics and Developmental Biology and an M.A. in Asian Studies/Japanese from University of Illinois. When she is not busy being a search geek, Shari is a die-hard Metallica fan, loves traveling to Iceland, and is not convinced that surfboards make great wall art. She resides in Elgin, Illinois.

Nick Musica has over 10 years experience designing, marketing, and managing websites. He's the founder of Think Green Media, an Internet marketing firm that offers search engine optimization, search marketing, web design, and web usability services.

He holds a B.A. in Communication with a concentration in Public Relations and Journalism from Monmouth University and an M.A. in Graphic Communications Management and Technology from New York University (NYU), where he lecturers on web design, search engine marketing, and web usability. He's also a Certified Usability Analyst (CUA).

Nick has designed and marketed websites for businesses in the fields of alternative energy, cosmetics, education, healthcare, finance, the nonprofit sector, retail, technology, and telecom. He's also a speaker to marketers and business owners on the topics of web design, search marketing, web usability, writing for the web, and search usability.

When he isn't working on search usability, you can find Nick surfing in the Atlantic Ocean or playing mediocre renditions of '80s and '90s songs on his ukulele. For those wondering: Yes, there is surf in New Jersey, yes, surfing in mid-February can sometimes get just a little cold, and yes, surfboards make great wall art.

■ CONTRIBUTORS

Technical Editors

Anne F. Kennedy is a managing partner and founder of Beyond Ink. With nearly 40 years' experience in marketing and public relations, Anne founded Beyond Ink in 1997 to bring the fundamental principles of marketing communications to online media. A search engine marketer for more than 10 years, she is an industry thought leader, sought-after speaker, and writer worldwide.

Currently, Anne represents professional SEO firms on the Search Engine Strategies (SES) Domestic Advisory Board, an influential group of business professionals from various industries and fields of expertise selected to propel the search industry forward.

In 2001 she launched SEOnews.net to foster better understanding of the emerging search marketing platform and opportunities to a growing market of potential customers.

Beyond Ink uses ethical principles of effective marketing communications to achieve critical third-party endorsements in popular, highly visible portals such as Google, MSN, Yahoo, and other top search media for clients, which include large household name brands as well as many small businesses, nonprofits, and online start-ups.

Anne resides in Maine and Oregon, but can always be found at Beyondink.com.

John Sorflaten founded Optimum Performance Training in 1985 after filing several patent applications on a Japanese word processing input system. His design recommendations dramatically reduced the keyboard learning process through user-centered design. He then moved into designing usable interfaces as a response to his question "Why train, when you can design it to be usable right away?"

John accumulated 20 years of consulting and teaching experience with the largest worldwide user-interface consulting firm, Human Factors International (HFI). He taught hundreds of courses supporting certification as a Usability Analyst since the inception of the program at HFI (www.humanfactors.com).

Since 1992, John has been a Certified Professional Ergonomist, the top professional certification for usability. He fills demands as a public speaker, writer, and innovator in social-web and rich interface applications. His redesign of www.ninds.nih.gov won a Best of the Fed award.

With a degree in Cinema from the University of Southern California and a Ph.D. in Instructional Design, John provides clients with seasoned advice and user research. This specialization ensures effective integration of video, text, images, and brand moxie for websites.

Cover Photography

Francois Roux focuses his photography on nature, particularly in Central Park in New York City. Living in New York has provided him the unique opportunity to photograph natural settings and then to step immediately into an urban landscape of unique and historic architecture. His pictures of France have often focused on black and white images of the mountains of Hautes Alpes, the region of southeastern France where he was raised.

When Shari and Nick asked Francois to contribute a cover photograph for this book, his inclination was to use an architectural image to suggest the convergence of search and usability. What better place to find such an image than at the Rose Center for Earth and Space at New York's American Museum of Natural History? The building's contained sphere, itself containing the planetarium, is surfaced in a mesh-like pattern of intersecting rays and concentric circles. This visual pattern lends itself to two-dimensional representation while still suggesting three-dimensional structure. You can see more of his photography at: francois-roux-photography.com.

Cartoons

Ron Leishman is an illustrator/cartoonist and owner of Toonaday.com and ToonClipart.com.

Ron has worked as an illustrator for over 20 years. His work has appeared in greeting cards, magazines, and newspapers, where he worked as an editorial cartoonist for a number of years. Along the way he has created a number of logos for new companies.

Earlier in his career, Ron also was co-creator of Captain Canuck, who was published in comic book form for a number of years in the '70s and '80s.

With the advent of the Internet, Ron moved to the web in 1996 with his site Toonaday.com, for which he has drawn a daily cartoon for the past 13 years and to which he continues to contribute on a daily basis. Recently, he has expanded his offerings with another website called ToonClipart.com.

Ron is a resident of Calgary, Alberta, and can be contacted at ron@toonclipart.com.

■ ACKNOWLEDGMENTS

This book took years of testing and experience to create. It also took the knowledge and support of some very important people.

Thank you to those directly involved in the creation of this book. To the staff at Peachpit Press—Nancy Peterson and Robyn Thomas for managing this project, for being great sounding boards, and for giving gentle nudges to keep things going. A special thanks goes to Michael Nolan and Doug Adrianson for continuing to work with us on multiple book projects. Thank you to the production and marketing staff at Peachpit for helping to shape this book and getting it out into the world.

We extend our heart-felt gratitude to Anne Kennedy and John Sorflaten, our technical editors, for their much valued feedback and suggestions. Your unique perspectives and encouraging comments on the chapters helped to focus the writing during late-night jam sessions.

To Francois Roux, thank you for the many photographs you took during the cover conception phase and for the final photograph that appears on the cover. To Ron Leishman, thank you for bringing the stories in this book to life with your illustrations and for injecting the book with your distinctive brand of visual humor.

Thank you to our colleagues whose work with web usability, search usability, search engine optimization, web design and development, copywriting, information architecture, and more have helped lay the groundwork for books like this. It's your work, some of which is referenced in this book, we recommend to clients, colleagues, and students.

Shari Thurow would like to personally thank her co-author, Nick Musica. Years ago, I knew I needed a co-author to address this complex but fascinating topic. I remember constantly saying to you, "Keep writing things down. I know you will use these experiences some time in the future." Thank you for taking my advice and for being one of my most valued friends and colleagues.

I would also like to thank the folks at Incisive Media and Search Marketing Expo—Karen DeWeese, Chris Elwell, Stewart Quealy, and Marilyn Crafts—for providing me with a venue to present this topic. You have been wonderful, supportive colleagues and friends.

My success in this industry clearly lies with the existence of the commercial web search engines and their vast knowledge of information retrieval and search usability. I extend my heartfelt thanks to my search engine colleagues—Matt Cutts, Jon Glick, Amit Kumar, Tim Mayer, Priyank Garg, Rajat Mukherjee, Amit Singhal, Bryan White, and Michael Yang.

And finally, my sincerest gratitude goes to the four people who inspire me to continue my lifelong foray into search usability: Danny Sullivan, Chris Sherman, Susan Weinschenk, and Peter Morville. A chance online meeting with Danny in the mid 1990s inspired me to pursue search-engine-friendly web design. And both Susan's and Peter's work inspired me to pursue website usability and information architecture as important elements of search-engine-friendly web design.

Nick Musica would like to personally thank his friend, colleague, and co-author Shari Thurow. You are a true inspiration and a pleasure to work with. Thank you for your generosity and for inviting me to take this ride with you.

Thank you to those indirectly involved in the creation of this book. To my clients and employers along the way who have given me their trust. It's because of your faith in my abilities that I have been able to grow and learn professionally from the experiences.

I've been fortunate to work with many people whose influence has helped shape my professional life. The list is long, but at the top are Andy Fischler, Tracy Wehringer, Nick Valente, Marc Buro, Cle Scouten, Bonnie Blake, and Shari Thurow.

Thank you to my family and friends whose phone calls, emails, and texts were returned later than I would have liked. Thank you for your understanding, support, and the occasional healthy distraction during the writing of this book. Thank you to those who shared in the life experiences used to relate some of the concepts in this book. Thank you to those across the border who helped me get away, even if it was just for the day. And thank you to those on two and four legs who dropped by to see how things were going and let me know when the Atlantic was calling.

And last but not least, to users who aren't afraid to "think out loud," thank you for showing me what only you can show.

■ CONTENTS AT A GLANCE

■ CONTENTS

■ FOREWORD

In the heart of the Yorkshire Dales in Northern England, a pleasant wander leads through the woods from Bolton Abbey to the Strid, a notorious stretch of water where the River Wharfe is forced into a deep and narrow channel. At its narrowest point, the Strid is about two metres (or a lengthy stride) wide, just right to tempt a daring child or a reckless adult. But, jumping the gap is risky, for the rocks are slippery, and nobody survives a fall into the thundering waters and deep, dark caverns of the Strid.

I'm reminded of this chasm not crossed when I ponder the state of search, a vast sociosemantic territory that's riddled with potholes, gaps, and schisms. Many of these fissures are carved by the relentless process of specialization. Designers, developers, information architects, search engine optimization specialists, and web analyticists are valued for their unique strengths, but their singular skills often come with a narrow focus and an idiosyncratic vocabulary that makes teamwork difficult at best.

And, of course, this collaboration chasm creates an experience gap that frustrates users to no end. Our expectations, raised high by Google, are all too often shattered by the sad state of site search. And, as the deep web grows ever more vast and unruly, even mighty Google cannot keep pace. The gulf between people and the answers they seek threatens to widen, and it's for this reason that this book that you hold in your hands is so vital to the future of findability.

Shari Thurow is among the few specialists brave enough to bridge the gap between search engine optimization and web usability. As a result, she has learned how and where to place stepping stones and build bridges. She can speak the language of link analysis and relevance ranking algorithms, while also understanding user psychology and information-seeking behavior. In this book, Shari and her co-author Nick Musica explain how you can design websites that are friendly to spiders and humans, so that even novice users can find the site and find their way around the site without plunging headfirst into the abyss.

So, if you're crazy enough to leap the Strid alone, it's ready and waiting. But, if you'd prefer a safer path across the chasm, then read this book. See you on the other side!

—Peter Morville

Author of *Ambient Findability: What We Find Changes Who We Become* (O'Reilly Publishing, 2005) and *Information Architecture for the World Wide Web*, 3rd Edition (O'Reilly Publishing, 2006).

INTRODUCTION

Why is this book needed?

In the United States alone, users submit more than 10 billion searches a month on commercial search engines such as Google, Yahoo, and MSN. Many of these searches leave users frustrated because what they find on search engine results pages and on resulting websites doesn't meet the expectations of their search queries. This means a poor experience for users and lost revenue for website owners.

So, what's the problem? The problem isn't the users or their queries. It's not the commercial search engines either. We are the problem—search engine optimizers, web usability professionals, web designers and developers, information architects and copywriters and other web professionals whose work either helps users find what they are looking for or doesn't. We are also the solution.

This book covers how users look for information and how search engines anticipate the intent behind users' queries so that we can work collectively to bridge the gap between what users search for on search engines and what they find on our websites. In short, it's your work that can improve the user experience and increase revenue by getting the right user to the right content if you understand the intent behind a user's query and the many ways users search for information on the web.

This book also provides a common language for web professionals from various backgrounds to use so we can better communicate with each other. For example, when you hear someone talking about a *navigational query* you'll know that they are talking about a user trying to locate a specific website using a commercial search engine. When you hear someone say they saw someone *pogo-sticking* on a website, you know they were referring to a user's search behavior and not to someone actually using a pogo stick.

It takes many web professionals, from multiple disciplines, to get the right user to the right content. Users don't know this, nor do they care. They just want to find their content. This book will help you get users to their content and meet business goals with the same user click.

■ WHO SHOULD READ THIS BOOK?

This book is for search engine optimization professionals, web usability professionals, web designers, web copywriters, web developers, online marketers, brand managers, website owners, management, and anyone who wants to improve their users' experience and increase revenue.

The main intended audience for *When Search Meets Web Usability* is search engine optimization (SEO) professionals who want to go beyond achieving page one rankings to creating a better experience for their users that also contributes to the bottom line of the business. For these SEO pros, this book will be valuable for self-education and as a reference book.

This book will assist SEO professionals in accomplishing the *how* of search engine optimization by explaining why search engines serve up the results they do and understanding the various behaviors users exhibit as they look for information on the web.

We have sprinkled resources throughout these pages for those who wish to educate themselves on web usability and search usability topics that go beyond the focus of *When Search Meets Web Usability*.

Web usability professionals are the second target audience. Web usability professionals will most likely be familiar with many of the concepts discussed in *When Search Meets Web Usability*. What you will find here that you haven't seen in other usability books is how to apply your skills and background beyond the websites to where many times the user experience really begins—the search engines. This book is meant to supplement your current usability methodologies and practices by showing how you can apply your knowledge of human factors to web users' querying behaviors on the commercial search engines.

Web usability professionals will also see topics they aren't familiar with that are of a search engine optimization nature and are critical to understanding how users behave when they query on the commercial search engines.

The third target audience includes, but is not limited to, web designers and developers, information architects, copywriters, and other web professionals. If you perform one or more of these roles, this book is meant to complement your background and supplement your skills by providing another perspective of the web and how your work affects users and the bottom line.

■ INGREDIENTS TO MAKE YOUR OWN SECRET SAUCE

There is no off-the-shelf *secret sauce* that this or any other book can offer you that will magically make your website number one in the commercial search engines, make users love your site, and make you millions of dollars.

What we can offer you instead are the ingredients to make your own secret sauce. All of the ingredients are in the pages of this book. They include understanding how search engines anticipate the intent of users, what influences users to click on your listing in the search engine results pages (SERPs), and understanding the many behaviors users exhibit when they search for information in the SERPs and on your website. It also includes something that strings everything together, called the *scent of information*.

FIGURE i.1 When it comes to a *secret sauce*, some like it hot, some like it not. You need to season your website to your users' taste.

By using these ingredients, you'll be able to create a unique recipe that will serve your users and your clients or employers better than any generic secret sauce ever could. We'll show you how.

■ WHAT YOU'LL LEARN

- The *how* and *why* of search engine optimization return on investment (ROI)
- Why Google doesn't want your site to be number one and what to do about it
- What makes a user click a SERP listing and how you can use that knowledge for profit
- The behaviors users exhibit when they look for information on the web
- How one user's click can both satisfy user goals and increase your revenue

■ WHERE DID THE RESEARCH IN THIS BOOK COME FROM?

The three query types (navigational, informational, and transactional queries) covered in this book originated from research by engineers at commercial search engines such as Google, Yahoo, and MSN. Since commercial search engines started using these query types they have been widely written about in academic circles but have never been presented for consumption to search optimization professionals, web usability professionals, and other web professionals in the context of search usability and in the detail in which they are covered in this book.

Additional research was adapted from the web usability profession. We've taken concepts and practices of web usability that historically only have been applied to websites and have applied them to how users use commercial search engines. We've also applied these concepts and practices to the websites that users find via a search engine query to show how we can improve the entire user experience starting with the query and finishing on your website.

Finally, you will see that some of the content in this book comes from our personal experience. We'd like to note that when we write from our personal experience we are not writing from our personal preference, but from our professional experience observing users and their behavior. We all have opinions, but this book is not about opinions; it's about understanding user behavior by distinguishing fact from opinions. Even *our* opinions.

■ HOW TO USE THIS BOOK

We suggest you read this book from beginning to end regardless of your experience as an SEO professional, usability professional, or other web professional; each chapter builds on concepts covered in previous chapters.

Chapters 1 through 6 define search usability terminology including information scent, the three types of queries that search engines use to anticipate the intent of a user's search, and the behaviors users exhibit on the web. The concepts and vocabulary defined in Chapters 1 through 6 are necessary to understand Chapters 7 through 9, which illustrate the return on investment of search usability, how different web professionals help or hurt search usability, and how you can get one-on-one direct feedback from your users by conducting web usability tests.

If you are a web usability professional, a glance at the this book's table of contents might tempt you to skip certain chapters. Don't skip chapters that look familiar to you, as they contain something new. We've taken concepts that many of you are familiar with and applied them to how users query on the web. So, while concepts such as eye tracking, functional salience tests, and expectancy tests might be familiar, how they are applied in the context of search usability most likely won't be.

■ WWW.SEARCH-MEETS-USABILITY.COM

We've supplemented this book with a companion site located at www.search-meets-usability.com. Here you will find:

- A list of resources for you to continue your search usability education
- Microsoft Excel spreadsheets from Chapter 7
- Content that didn't make it into the book due to publishing limitations
- Additional content, resulting from feedback we get from readers like yourself
- A growing glossary of search usability terminology for you to reference, recommend to colleagues, and use to communicate with other web professionals

CHAPTER 1

UNDERSTANDING SEARCH USABILITY

A user-friendly, search-friendly website benefits both site visitors and businesses. Site visitors easily find what they need, accomplish their goals, and leave satisfied. Businesses reap the benefits of a happy customer. However, search engine optimizers and website usability professionals focus on different aspects of search usability. By applying a holistic approach and merging the skills and widening the focus of both search engine optimizers and usability professionals, you can increase traffic, leads, sales, and happy customers. But first, we need to understand what search actually means.

If you ask people to envision the word *search*, you will get a wide variety of responses. On the web, the word *search* has become synonymous with Google, as in, "I Googled his name to get some background information before we went on a date." Others envision a scene from a Sherlock Holmes story, perhaps an image of a bloodhound sniffing a crime scene for clues. To others, the word *search* is associated with misplaced keys and a scramble to locate them before leaving for work (**Figure 1.1**). Or even a scavenger hunt at a family picnic. Clearly, the meaning of *search* is multifaceted. Its meaning depends on its context—both online and offline.

Figure 1.1 Thinking that Google is the beginning and end of how people look for content on the web makes just as much sense as trying to use Google to find your keys.

■ DIFFERING PERSPECTIVES ON SEARCH

On the web, it is easy to see why the word *search* is associated with search engines only. The two main visual cues that communicate online searching are: a button labeled "Search" and a text box where searchers can describe their desired information, destination, or activity. Billions of searches are performed on Google, Yahoo, and Microsoft Live every month. Millions of websites have a site search engine. Therefore, considering the tremendous use of web and site searches, millions of people associate online searching with search engines. **Figure 1.2** and **Figure 1.3** are examples of two types of search engines. The interfaces for both websites contain a Search button and a text box.

Note A *web search engine,* such as Google, is a tool designed to discover, retrieve, analyze, and display information from the World Wide Web. On the other hand, a *site search engine* is a tool that retrieves, analyzes, and displays snippets of information about pages from a specific website.

Figure 1.2 Web search engine.

Figure 1.3 Site search engine.

However, people do not use only the commercial web search engines to look for content on the web. People might go to a specific web page after they remember a reference from newspaper, billboard, television show, radio program, or even word of mouth. They type the website address (URL) in an address bar (**Figure 1.4** and **Figure 1.5**).

FIGURE 1.4 The web address bar on the current Firefox browser (for laptop and desktop computers).

FIGURE 1.5 The web address bar on an Apple iPhone.

In addition, people might look for web content by clicking a link from an email, text message, or an online advertisement. They also locate web content by clicking links from one site to another, commonly known as *surfing* or *browsing* the web. When people look for content via these methods, they are still searching. When searching these other ways, we still "search" even though we don't see the familiar text entry box and Search button.

On the web, *search usability* refers to how easily users can locate and discover content on a site via retrieval (searching/querying) and navigation (browsing). Search usability also refers to users' level of satisfaction as they discover or locate their desired content. Therefore, to say a website is "usable" means that users find no obstacles in finding what they want. In fact, they actually get satisfaction from the process of finding what they want.

On the web, search usability *refers to how easily users can locate and discover content on a site via retrieval (searching/querying) and navigation (browsing).*

Because users locate and discover web content using multiple techniques, search usability addresses both browsing behavior—clicking a link from one web page to another—and querying behavior. People find web content in a wide variety of ways, not only via the commercial web search engines.

Search engine optimizers and usability professionals focus on different aspects of search usability (**Figure 1.6**). Let's look at what each practitioner focuses on.

FIGURE 1.6 Both search engine optimizers and website usability professionals only address part of search usability. Users exhibit all four behaviors.

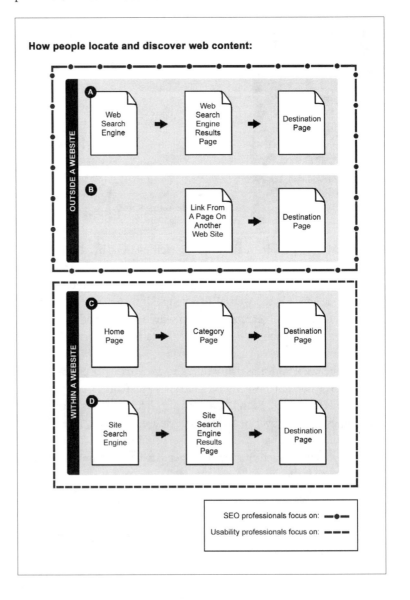

Search Engine Optimization (SEO)

Search engine optimization has traditionally been defined as the process of designing, writing, coding (in HTML), scripting, and programming an entire website so that there is a good chance that web-page listings will appear in top positions in web search results for selected keywords. Most people view SEO as an online marketing strategy. Many search engine optimizers focus on web search engine optimization (**Figure 1.7**) because they see SEO in the context of designing and writing web content for search engines, not for human beings.

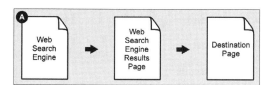

FIGURE 1.7 Many search engine optimizers focus on web search engine optimization.

Search engine optimization is not optimizing a website for search engines. Rather, SEO is optimizing a website for people who use search engines. There is a human element to SEO that usability professionals might not realize.

Understanding searchers and their goals is a large part of the optimization process. Search engine optimizers gather information about users with keyword research tools and web analytics data. Link popularity, or the more appropriate term *link development*, is one of the key building blocks of search engine optimization. Link development is the number and quality of external, third-party links pointing to a website. All the major web search engines use link popularity to determine positioning in search results pages. Therefore, the goal for most search engine optimizers is to assist website owners in obtaining high quality links (**Figure 1.8**).

NOTE An example of an objective third-party link from one website to another is a link on Wikipedia that leads to a web page that is not within the Wikipedia site, such as a link from http://en.wikipedia.org/wiki/National_cancer_institute to the official National Cancer Institute site at http://www.cancer.gov.

FIGURE 1.8 Search engine optimizers also focus on link development.

Search engine optimizers specialize in areas of search usability that usability professionals do not. Unlike usability professionals, for example, most search engine optimizers do not have one-to-one face time with actual users.

Now let's look at what usability professionals focus on.

Website Usability

Just as the word *search* elicits a wide variety of images and interpretations, so does the word *usability*. In fact, many people have never even heard of the word *usability*. If you ask the average person on the street or in an elevator what they believe *usability* means, you might get a confused expression in response. One common interpretation of the word is to break it down into two components, *use* and *ability*, resulting in the perceived definition of *usability* as a person's ability to use something. When referring to a website, people often think, "I can use my website. Therefore, it must be user friendly."

Unfortunately, this common interpretation of the word *usability* is incorrect, because, when it is applied to a website, usability has nothing to do with personal opinion. Website usability is task-oriented. Through usability testing, usability professionals measure how well users can accomplish specific tasks on a website with efficiency and a high level of satisfaction.

NOTE For a more detailed explanation of website usability, see http://www.w3.org/WAI/redesign/ucd.

During usability testing on a website, usability professionals measure:

- **Effectiveness.** Can site visitors achieve what they need from using your website? Can they easily find their desired information, destination, or activity?

- **Efficiency.** How quickly can site visitors complete their goals on your website? How many steps are required to complete basic tasks? What elements on a site discouraged or prevented site visitors from achieving their goals?

- **Learnability.** How quickly and easily can new site visitors learn to use your website? What elements on a site can help site visitors form an accurate mental model of your site?

- **Memorability.** How quickly and easily can repeat site visitors remember how to use your website effectively to accomplish their goals?

- **Error prevention and recovery.** No website is 100 percent error-free. Does the website implement a design that allows for easy recovery from errors?

- **Satisfaction.** User satisfaction is heavily influenced by the ability to achieve goals. If site visitors are able to achieve their goals on a website with ease and efficiency, they report high satisfaction. If site visitors encounter too many roadblocks, they report low satisfaction, even if they were able to accomplish their goals. Would a test participant recommend the website to others?

Good website usability is not the same as people saying they like or use your site. Focus group opinions bear little resemblance to actual behaviors exhibited during usability tests. Because they do not wish to appear stupid in front of a group, people downplay problems and issues with a site. They will say that they like a site even though they are unable to find their desired content. People are not always objective when evaluating their own behavior.

Usability professionals recognize the value of one-on-one interaction with actual users through usability testing and field studies. They see firsthand that a positive user experience does not come from a brand manager's perspective, a marketing manager's perspective, management's perspective, or even an SEO professional's perspective. Positive user experiences come from observing users' successful completion of a task, and not solely from users saying that they felt good about it. Usability professionals focus on search usability when users are already on a website, usually beginning at a home page (**Figure 1.9**). Usability professionals do not always consider how users actually arrive on a site.

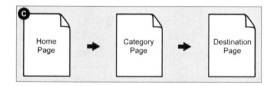

FIGURE 1.9 Usability tests are conducted on a website, typically beginning with a home page.

Finally, in the website usability industry, the term *search usability* is typically used to describe the user-friendliness of a site search engine (**Figure 1.10**). What both search engine optimizers and usability professionals might not realize is that the techniques search engine optimizers use often make site search results more accurate. In other words, many web SEO techniques make site search results more accurate because page content becomes more keyword focused.

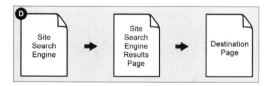

FIGURE 1.10 Usability tests are conducted on a website, including tests on a site search engine.

Problems arise when search engine optimizers and usability professionals work against each other, sometimes without even realizing it. For example, many search engine optimizers put so many keywords on a web page that the page becomes unusable. On the flip side, in the name of reducing the amount of text on a page, many usability professionals remove important keywords from web pages, making them appear unfocused to both site visitors and search engines. The result? The user experience and business goals are compromised.

Findability expert Peter Morville eloquently stated that people cannot use what they cannot find. Search engine optimization professionals help make content easy to find via the commercial web search engines. Website usability professionals help make content easy to find on a website. The string that connects these two groups is the scent of information. People need the scent of information in order to locate and discover desired content. Let's explore what we mean by the *scent of information* next.

> **NOTE** See http://www.findability.org/archives/cat_findability.php for the link to Peter Morville's statement.

> **NOTE** The concept of the *scent of information* comes from information foraging theory by Peter Pirolli, Stuart Card, and colleagues at the Palo Alto Research Center. See *Information Foraging Theory: Adaptive Interaction with Information* (New York, NY: Oxford University Press, 2007).

■ THE SCENT OF INFORMATION

A web page consists of many graphical and textual cues that facilitate navigation (where can I go?), orientation (where am I?), and assessment of content value (should I click this link?). These words and images are the *scent of information*. If the scent of information is strong, people click. If the scent of information is too weak or disappears, people do not click. To make web content findable, information scents should be clearly established and consistently maintained throughout a website.

If the scent of information is strong, people click.

We react to various information scents in our everyday life without even realizing it. For example, when you ride in an elevator, the elevator buttons and lights provide a scent of information. If you press the button labeled "3," the elevator will take you to the third floor. If you press the button labeled "5," the elevator will take you to the fifth floor. If you press the button labeled "Lobby," the elevator will take you to the lobby.

> **NOTE** On a website, *orientation* is a behavior whereby users determine their position with reference to another point, establishing a "sense of place." For example, locational breadcrumb links help people understand where they are in the hierarchy of a website, such as Home > Teas > Green Teas. Orientation will be discussed in detail in Chapter 6, "The Scent of Information and Landing Pages."

Sometimes, though, the scent of information on elevators is not clear. The following photographs and illustrations show two sets of elevator buttons from the same building. In Elevator 1, shown in **Figure 1.11**, if you wanted to go to the lobby, which button would you push?

When we observed people using the set of buttons in Elevator 1, they had confused expressions on their faces and hesitated to push a button. They were unsure which button would lead them to the lobby.

Most of them assumed that the buttons labeled 1R or 1F were the two best options, but they were unsure what the abbreviations "R" and "F" represented.

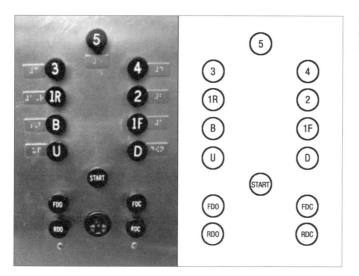

FIGURES 1.11 In Elevator 1, the scent of information to the lobby is weak and confusing.

Some people mentioned that the lobby is not always on the first floor and were ready to press either the button labeled B or D. However, they assumed that the letter "B" was the abbreviation for the basement, which confused them even more. No one knew what the letter "D" represented.

Ultimately, many of them said aloud, "Which one goes to the lobby?"

Interestingly, in the same building, a different situation was available in Elevator 2, shown in **Figures 1.12**. If you want to go to the lobby and are riding in Elevator 2, the correct button to push is more obvious.

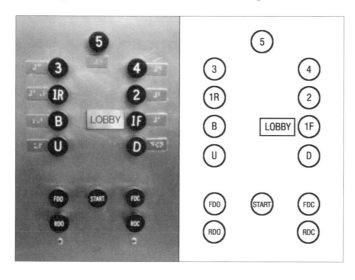

FIGURES 1.12 In Elevator 2, the scent of information to the lobby is very clear.

NOTE According to Gestalt Principles of Visual Organization, items placed close to each other are associated with each other. This is called the Principle of Proximity. See http://www.interaction-design.org/encyclopedia/gestalt_principles_of_form_perception.html.

When we observed people using the set of buttons in Elevator 2, there was no hesitation. There were no questions. People pressed the button labeled 1F because they correctly determined that pressing that button would get them to the lobby due to the strong scent information. Two items, in particular, established the scent of information: the word "Lobby" and its placement near the elevator button that will take them to the lobby.

Another item that communicates a strong scent of information is a map you might find in a shopping mall, or a mall directory, shown in **Figure 1.13**:

FIGURE 1.13 The scent of information on this mall directory contains both graphical and textual cues to help mall visitors establish where they are and where they can go.

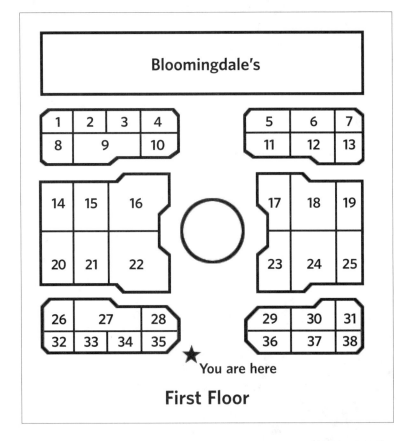

This diagram helps people understand where they are located within the mall. There is a graphical cue (a star) with a corresponding text label, "You are here." Another text label, "First Floor," lets them know what floor they are on.

Additionally, this mall directory shows people where they can go in multiple ways. People do not enter and exit a shopping mall through a single entry point. Shopping malls have multiple entrances. Many shopping malls have multiple wings, and there might be a main entrance for each wing. People can enter and exit a shopping mall via individual stores as well (such as the Bloomingdale's store shown in Figure 1.13).

Websites are similar to shopping malls in that they have multiple entry and exit points. When people arrive at a website, they do not always land on a home page, especially if they are coming from a web search engine. They might land on a page in the middle of a site. Site visitors need to see the textual and graphical cues that comprise the scent of information on a web page. If they don't, then they abandon a site. Let's look at a before-and-after example from the National Library of Medicine.

Back in 2002, the National Library of Medicine's home page looked like **Figure 1.14**:

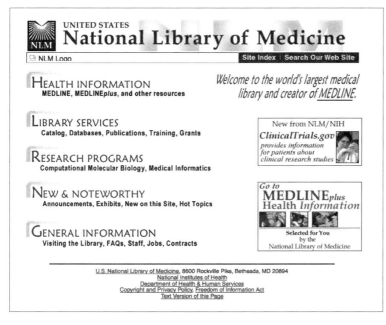

The scent of information provided on this home page might be effective for medical librarians but not for other site visitors. For example, what are MEDLINE and MEDLINE*plus*? These items appear multiple times on this home page as text and graphic images, but why are these items important to site visitors? Why would a person who wants health information click either of these links? Since this page provides little information about the value of the link, people are not as likely to continue to navigate the site for health information. Furthermore, the text links under the Health Information do not look clickable.

Now let's look at the revised version of the National Library of Medicine's home page in **Figure 1.15**.

FIGURE 1.15 The new home page provides more effective information scents for both users and search engines.

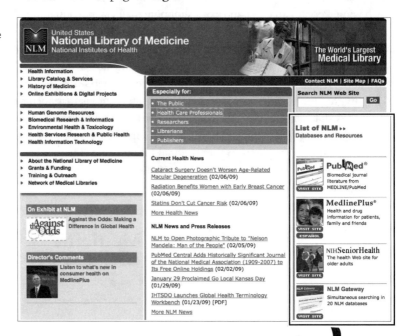

The revised home page provides more effective information scents for both site visitors and search engines. Now people who are unfamiliar with MEDLINE*plus* understand what they can learn by clicking the link. The MEDLINE*plus* graphic includes explanatory text, and people can get health and drug information for patients, family, and friends. This portion of the website is clearly written for consumers, not medical professionals. The photograph of people who are not medical professionals and the additional words in the annotation provide a stronger scent of information for all site visitors: laypersons, librarians, and medical professionals than the word MEDLINE*plus*. The additional words, in particular, also help make web pages more search-engine-friendly.

> **NOTE** The photograph is a good choice for the scent of information because women typically make healthcare decisions in a family. If a section of this website were targeting medical professionals, a photo of a physician, nurse, a person wearing a lab coat, or a group of these people would be a good choice.

WHY SEARCH USABILITY IS IMPORTANT

As we mentioned in the introduction, a user-friendly, search-friendly website benefits both site visitors and businesses. The primary benefits to site visitors are that they are able to achieve their goals easily, efficiently, and with a high degree of satisfaction. The primary benefits for businesses are increased traffic, qualified leads, closed sales, and happy customers.

Ignoring or minimizing search usability can result in substantial costs to a business not only in terms of lost sales and prospects, but also in terms of customer satisfaction, increased advertising expenses, and staff time. Websites with content that is difficult to find can result in the following business costs:

- **If people find it difficult to locate or discover their desired content, they will not use your site.**

  Whenever people make a choice, they tend to pick the easiest option. This is especially common on the web, where a more user-friendly website is only one or two clicks away.

  If people believe a website does not contain their desired content, they will quickly abandon the site. They will not *Add to cart*. They will not write a product review. They will not join your online community. Moreover, they are unlikely to return to the site, remembering it as the site that delivered a poor user experience because:

  - They could not locate their desired content at all.
  - The website made it very difficult to locate their desired content.
  - The content they found was not what they expected or wanted.

- **If people feel they must use a website where desired content is difficult to find, they will use the site as little as possible.**

  If a website is not user-friendly, site visitors will go to great lengths to avoid using the site, even if they believe the desired content is outstanding. Site visitors often create elaborate workarounds to avoid using the website, and will share these workarounds with others.

  For example, it is not uncommon to see people use Google to go directly to a specific page within a website, because the site's navigation scheme is too confusing or the URL (web address) is too complex.

- **If people have a difficult time finding desired content on your site, they will waste time.**

  A website that is not user-friendly and search-friendly will make site visitors hunt for their desired information unnecessarily. Site visitors will take longer to learn how to use your website, and any tasks that they do not perform regularly will take longer to complete, resulting in more errors.

- **The website will need more changes and enhancements.**

  If searchers' needs and abilities were not considered when determining the requirements, design, and programming of a website, then the site is likely to require more changes and enhancements. Result? Businesses must allocate more staff and/or more staff time to a website to fix problems that should have been addressed before the site was launched.

■ CONCLUSION

Key points in this chapter:

- On the web, the word *search* is associated with search engines because of a button labeled "Search" and a text box where people can describe their desired information, destination, or activity.

- *Search usability* refers to how well users can locate and discover content on a website via retrieval (searching/querying) and navigation (browsing) in order to achieve their goals on the web.

- Search engine optimizers and website usability professionals focus on different aspects of search usability.

- Search engine optimization (SEO) is not designing and writing a site for search engines. Best practice SEO is optimizing a website for *people who use search engines*.

- Search engine optimizers focus on both querying and browsing behaviors before people arrive on a website. Usability professionals focus on querying and browsing behaviors after people arrive on a website.

- Website usability is task oriented. Through usability testing, usability professionals measure how well users can accomplish specific tasks with efficiency and a high level of satisfaction.

- Website usability is about effectiveness, efficiency, learnability, memorability, error prevention, and satisfaction. It is not a set of focus group opinions.

- People cannot use what they cannot find, in the words of Peter Morville.

- The string that connects website usability professionals and search engine optimizers is the scent of information.

- The scent of information consists of graphical and textual cues that facilitate navigation (where can I go?), orientation (where am I?), and assessment of content value (should I click this link?).

- To make web content findable, make your information irresistibly meaningful and consistent in its allure throughout your website.

CHAPTER 2

THE SCENT OF INFORMATION AND WEB SEARCH ENGINES

People use commercial web search engines for a wide variety of reasons. They might want to look up a phone number or get directions to a restaurant. They might want to read consumer reviews before purchasing an item. Or they might want to play a quick game of Sudoku online.

So, to help searchers succeed in getting what they want, savvy marketers must understand: *how* people are searching, and *why* people are searching. Once marketers know the answers to these questions, they can adjust their search marketing strategies. Not only will their websites receive increased traffic, they will also receive more *qualified* traffic that results in higher conversions, sales, and lifetime customers (**Figure 2.1**).

FIGURE 2.1 Both search engine marketers and usability professionals can get a higher return on investment if they understand how and why people search. They can use that knowledge to build more user-friendly websites.

HOW + WHY = ROI

people search   people search   (return on investment)

If many search engine marketers were fishermen, they just might starve. While a fisherman's gear might help attract multiple types of fish, there is no one-size-fits-all gear in the tackle box (**Figure 2.2**). Fishermen have multiple rods, reels, and bait to choose from depending on what type of fish they wish to catch. It is the type of fish that determines the gear the fisherman uses.

FIGURE 2.2 Ranking well on a web search engine is pointless if you are reaching the wrong target audience.

Likewise, it is the type of searcher that determines the marketing strategies that search engine optimization (SEO) professionals use. Is the target audience novice, intermediate, or advanced searchers? What are their main goals? Searchers can be characterized by experience level, plus their goals and behaviors. When people use the commercial web search engines, they are trying to communicate where they want to go, what they want to read, and what they want to do.

When people use the commercial web search engines, they are trying to communicate where they want to go, what they want to read, and what they want to do.

Knowledgeable SEO professionals continually try to understand the goals and characteristics of web searchers. With this knowledge, they can help site owners build web pages that meet user expectations and satisfy their needs. To do this, they use the *scent of information*—the keywords that people type into search engines.

By increasing the scent of information using the keywords in search listings, site owners can encourage users to click their listings and maintain their site's search engine visibility, meeting both business objectives and users' expectations. The scent of information is a key way to convince web searchers to bite and to keep them hooked.

In this chapter, we'll explore querying as a positive search behavior and explain some of its negative perceptions. We will also go over the main components of a web page's search listing and learn where the commercial web search engines are getting this information.

NOTE On the web, a *query* is typically defined as a question or a request for information. If you are speaking with a web search expert, the word *querying* is more accurate than the word *searching* for describing the primary activity associated with search engines (such as typing words into a search box).

■ DIFFERENT PERCEPTIONS OF QUERYING BEHAVIOR

As mentioned previously, SEO professionals view querying as a positive search behavior because people are communicating where they want to go, what they want to read, and what they want to do. People do not always know what content is available on prospective websites. They use a web search engine to discover new content.

Additionally, people might remember great content they read or used previously. They might not have bookmarked the web page. They might not have printed or written the name of the site or its URL. So they use a web search engine to re-find that desirable content.

Keywords are a user-generated scent of information.

Therefore, SEO professionals view querying behavior as a positive search behavior. From their perspective, query formulation is an opportunity to present searchers with desired content. The users' scent of information is unmistakable—it consists of the keywords that people type into search engines. In other words, keywords are a user-generated scent of information.

Usability professionals, on the other hand, have different perceptions of querying behavior. They often observe users' frustration and confusion with search engines and search engine results pages (SERPs). They also observe site abandonment—points at which users leave a website—due to querying behavior. To them, querying behavior can signify a diminished, or missing, scent of information.

So whose perception is more accurate? Let's look at some of these perceptions individually to see how these two groups differ, and to see what they have in common.

Missing Information Scent

A *site search*, not to be confused with a *web search*, is a secondary navigational aide. During usability testing on a site, participants tend not to use a site search engine (**Figure 2.3**) until they're unable to find information by browsing. If users do not see keywords in the web page, they resort to using a site search engine to find what they want and to create the missing information scent. Therefore, for usability professionals, querying behavior is a negative search behavior—a failure of site navigation.

Figure 2.3 Users might use a site search engine if they are unable to find desired content via browsing. Therefore, site querying is often viewed as a negative search behavior in usability terms.

However, on a *web* search engine (**Figure 2.4**), querying is viewed as a positive search behavior because searchers are communicating what they desire.

FIGURE 2.4 Web search engine experts view querying as a positive search behavior.

Irrelevant or Poor Search Results

Many web content creators have commercial motives for achieving top web search engine positions, regardless of how relevant they are to the user's request. How many times have you Googled a person's name and seen some rather odd search listings? How many times have you clicked a link from Google and landed on a web page (**Figure 2.5**) that did not have the information you wanted? And how many times have you abandoned a website because the information you found simply wasn't want you had in mind when you began your query?

FIGURE 2.5 The reaction you don't want after a searcher clicks a link to your website from Google.

Usability professionals commonly observe this user frustration and confusion. Usability professionals also experience this frustration personally when they use a commercial web search engine. From a usability perspective, they do not recognize the critical balance between business goals and user expectations. They see too much focus on business goals at the expense of a positive user experience.

Unfortunately, some web content creators and SEO professionals go to extreme measures to achieve top search engine positions. Search engine spam—which is creating pages deliberately to trick the web search engines into offering inappropriate, redundant, or poor-quality search results—is still used as a search engine marketing strategy. As a result, some substandard and irrelevant listings constantly appear at the top of Google or any search engine results. These substandard listings lead to a negative user experience for the search engine.

However, not all SEO professionals are search engine spammers. Many SEO professionals are dedicated to meeting user expectations—delivering and maintaining an appropriate information scent, beginning with the search listings on a search engine results page and ending on a website. These SEO professionals not only achieve top search engine positions, they also contribute positively to brand perception and brand affinity by appropriately matching user queries to web page content, resulting in more first-time visitors and more repeat visitors.

NOTE Search engine spam is still a common marketing strategy. Google and the other web search engines are constantly discovering and removing spam content. Check out Part 5, "Best Practices: Dos and Don'ts of Search Engine Optimization," in *Search Engine Visibility* (New Riders, 2007), for details about different types of search engine spam.

■ HOW TO PROVIDE INFORMATION SCENT IN SEARCH LISTINGS

A user-generated scent of information begins at the commercial web search engines when searchers type their query words into the search box. After users click the "Search" button, search engines validate the users' scent of information in search results by using *term highlighting*, which is highlighting, or bolding, the matching query words in the listing summaries. Search engines highlight query words in these places to help searchers feel more confident that they are seeing the best, most relevant listings. In **Figure 2.6**, you see term highlighting in both the (1) main search listings and (2) the ads in a Google SERP for the keyword phrase *thyroid cancer symptoms*.

NOTE A web page's search listing appears in the main content area of a search engine results page.

FIGURE 2.6 Search engines validate searchers' scent of information by highlighting query words, or keywords, in various places in the search engine results page (SERP).

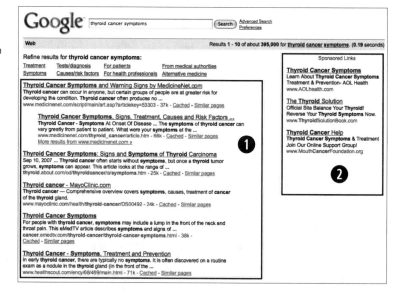

A good information scent has visible signs, which in the case of search results pages is term highlighting. For each main search listing, if query words are present, they are highlighted in the (1) title-tag content, (2) meta-tag description or page snippet, and (3) URL (**Figure 2.7**).

FIGURE 2.7 An individual search listing for the keyword phrase *thyroid cancer symptoms*. Keywords are highlighted in the title tag, page snippet, and URL.

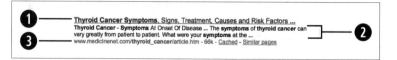

Searchers select the link that they feel provides the best scent of information. Each element (identified with a number in Figure 2.7) of a web page's search listing provides specific information scent. Let's look at each of these elements in detail.

Title Tags

An HTML title tag has a specific meaning to website design and search engines. The text between the `<title>` and `</title>` tags, is the web page title and is known as the *title tag*. It looks like:

`<title>The Art Institute of Chicago</title>`

On an actual web page in a web browser, title-tag content displays at the top of a screen (**Figure 2.8**).

Title-tag content

FIGURE 2.8 The title-tag content displays on browsers at the top of the screen.

Not only does the title-tag content validate and continue the users' scent of information, it also serves other purposes in the search listing:

- **Click-through** (**on the search listing**). The title-tag content is the call to action in each search listing. The title tag is formatted as a text link. Text links work best if they are between 7 and 12 words long, or approximately 40–69 characters, which is long enough to boost the chances of a searcher's query words appearing in a link, yet short enough to find the word easily while scanning the search results.

- **User confidence.** If keywords are present in the title tag, it increases user confidence. Searchers are more confident that search engines have delivered the best results when they see

NOTE See Jared Spool's report "Designing for the Scent of Information" at http://www.uie.com/reports/scent_of_information/.

NOTE Google gets title-tag content directly from each web page.

their query words displayed as a hyperlink. Searchers also believe clicking a keyword-focused link will lead them to desired content.

- **Relevancy.** All the major web search engines evaluate keyword use in title-tag content to calculate rankings.

Meta-Tag Description or Page Snippet

NOTE *On-the-page content* refers to content that is visible on a web browser between the <body> and </body> tags in XHTML code.

A search listing's description typically contains around 155 characters. Google gets the listing description from one of three places on a web page: meta-tag description, a single occurrence of on-the-page content, or multiple occurrences of on-the-page content.

The Art Institute's home page (Figure 2.8) only contains graphic images. Google and the other web search engines have a difficult time detecting what an image is and how to describe it. So they do not use text formatted in graphic images for a search listing. Instead, in this example, Google is displaying a portion of the meta-tag description as the search listing's description.

In source code, the meta-tag description looks like the following:

NOTE This meta-tag description contains approximately 270 characters, but Google only displays around 155 characters in the listing.

```
<meta name="description" content="The world-renowned Art
Institute of Chicago houses both a museum and school. The
museum contains more than 300,000 works of art while nearly
3,000 students are enrolled in various undergraduate and
graduate degree programs at the School of the Art Institute
of Chicago." />
```

For example, if you look at the Google listing of The Art Institute of Chicago's home page (**Figure 2.9**), you see that Google is generating the listing description from the meta-tag content.

FIGURE 2.9 Search listing for the query words *art institute*.

If a web page contains keywords in the on-the-page content area, Google might generate a listing description from *one part* of that content, as shown in **Figures 2.10** and **2.11**:

Snippet from page content

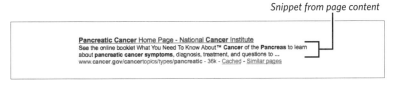

FIGURE 2.10 Search listing for the query words *pancreatic cancer symptoms.*

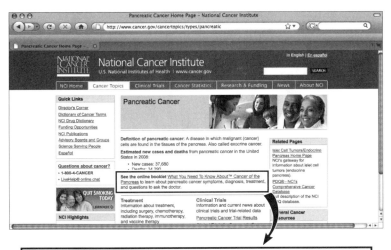

FIGURE 2.11 Landing page from the search listing shown in Figure 2.10. Google is generating this listing description from *one* snippet of text from the on-the-page content, even though the page has a meta-tag description.

Or, Google might generate a listing description from *multiple places* on a web page. If you look at the text in the search listing (in **Figure 2.12**) and compare it to the listing's landing page, you can see that Google is generating part of the listing description from two snippets (see **Figure 2.13** on the next page) and the meta-tag description.

Here is the source code for the meta-tag description:

```
<meta name="Description" content="NCI's gateway for
information about pancreatic cancer." />
```

And here is the Google listing:

Snippet from page content and meta-tag description

FIGURE 2.12 Search listing for the query words *pancreatic cancer trials.*

FIGURE 2.13 Landing page from the search listing shown in Figure 2.12. For the National Cancer Institute's Pancreatic Cancer page, Google is generating part of the listing description from *multiple snippets* of text from the on-the-page content.

TIP An important tip that warrants repeating: To ensure your search listings always contain a strong scent of information, keywords should be present in both on-the-page content and meta-tag descriptions

Google reserves the right to change listing descriptions to make them more useful for searchers. So no one knows exactly how a web page listing will appear in search results. Therefore, to ensure your search listings always contain a strong scent of information, keywords should be present in both on-the-page content and meta-tag descriptions.

URL Structure (Web Address)

In a search engine results page, the URL can be crucial for encouraging searchers to click the link to your web page because it can reinforce the scent of information. For example, let's look at the URL shown in Figure 2.13: http://www.cancer.gov/cancertopics/types/pancreatic

When we showed this URL, and only this URL, to usability test participants and asked them what they believed this web page is about, the answers were consistent:

- "It's a web page about pancreatic cancer topics."
- "It's about pancreatic cancer."
- "I can read information about the types of pancreatic cancer."

All participants correctly stated that the URL would lead them to a web page that contains information about pancreatic cancer. When we asked participants to come up with other web addresses that might help them understand the content that is available on that page, they came up with:

- www.cancer.gov/types/pancreatic.html
- www.cancer.gov/types/pancreas.html
- www.cancer.gov/cancer/pancreas.html
- www.cancer.gov/cancer/pancreatic.html
- www.cancer.gov/topics/pancreaticcancer.html
- www.cancer.gov/topics/pancreatic-cancer.html
- www.cancer.gov/cancertopics/pancreaticcancer.html
- www.cancer.gov/cancertopics/pancreatic-cancer.html
- www.cancer.gov/cancer/types/pancreatic.html
- www.cancer.gov/cancer/types/pancreas.html
- www.cancer.gov/pancreaticcancer.html
- www.cancer.gov/pancreatic-cancer.html
- www.cancer.gov/pancreatic.html
- www.cancer.gov/pancreas.html

All of these URLs provide a strong information scent because they contain important keywords. Additionally, some of these URLs are easier to read than others because they contain fewer characters.

TIP From a usability perspective, fewer characters in a URL makes it easier to read.

When we showed this next URL to test participants and asked them what they believed this web page was about

www.cancer.gov/cancertopics.aspx?ArticleId=1080

all test participants gave the same answer, "It's an article about cancer topic(s)." There was no mention of the keyword phrase *pancreatic cancer*. When we asked participants how confident they were that this URL would lead to a page about pancreatic cancer, most of them had doubts.

The following URL structure generated even less user confidence:

www.cancer.gov/cancertopics.aspx?CatId=1080&ArticleID=234

User confidence decreases when users do not see keywords in URLs. In an ideal situation, a web address provides useful information about a page's content.

Let's look at some parts of a sample URL where important keywords can be placed:

http://www.domain.com/subroot/path/file

- **Subroot:** A domain name followed by a single directory. In the following URL, the subroot is *brand*.
  http://www.company.com/brand/

- **Path:** A domain name followed by an arbitrarily deep path but not ending in the file name. In the following URL, the path name is *refrigerators*.
  http://www.company.com/brand/refrigerators/

- **File:** Anything ending in a file name other than *index.html*. In the following URL, the file name is *refrigerator-name.html*.
  http://www.company.com/brand/refrigerators/refrigerator-name.html

Every portion of a search listing is important for increased user confidence and clickability. If keywords are not present in a search listing, the information scent is very poor, and searchers are less likely to click the link in that listing. On the other hand, if there is too much bold text in a search listing, the listing becomes too hard to read—a big turn-off. Therefore, searchers are less likely to click that keyword-stuffed listing.

Every portion of a search listing is important for increased user confidence and clickability.

SEO professionals and site owners should maximize each of the three search listing elements for the desired impact. As you will see in forthcoming chapters, some portions of an individual search listing are more important than others. Which portion of a search listing is important for searchers who want to go to a specific website? Which portion of a search listing is important for searchers who want to do something?

Site owners should understand how the searcher's intent determines the importance of each search listing element.

■ 3 TYPES OF WEB SEARCH ENGINE QUERIES

Since 2002, web search queries have been classified based on searcher intent. (See Andrei Broder, "A taxonomy of web search," SIGIR Forum, 36(2) (2002): 3-10.) These three query types are called *navigational, informational,* and *transactional.* By understanding the three types of queries, SEO professionals can work with the search engines to serve up the right content to the right user for a specific query. The better you can anticipate the user's query intent, the better chance you have of meeting user goals and driving business via your website.

Note The article "A taxonomy of web search" is available online at: www.sigir.org/forum/F2002/broder.pdf.

- **Navigational queries** are ones in which the searcher wants to go to a specific website, or a specific web page (usually a home page) on a specific website. Approximately 10 to 26 percent of web search queries are navigational.

- **Informational queries** are ones in which the searcher wishes to read or view more information about a topic. Informational queries are the most common type of search engine query, comprising anywhere between 48 and 80 percent of web search queries.

- **Transactional queries** are ones in which the searcher wishes to perform some interaction on the web, aside from reading. Approximately 10 to 24 percent of web search queries are transactional.

By satisfying navigational, informational, and transactional query needs, website owners can get a higher return on investment (ROI) than by satisfying transactional queries alone.

To ensure your website is successful, you should make sure your website accommodates all query types. Users might perform multiple types of searches to find your website. For example, searchers might want to monitor a bid on an item for sale on eBay. Before searchers can monitor a bid (informational), they must first go to the eBay website (navigational).

By satisfying navigational, informational, and transactional query needs, website owners can get a higher return on investment (ROI) than by satisfying transactional queries alone. Therefore, it'll pay off if you address all query types when building and writing content for your websites. The next three chapters will cover the three query types in detail, but let's take a quick look at what user behaviors classify queries into each of these categories.

Navigational Queries

As shown in **Figure 2.14**, searchers have a variety of options to accomplish the task of navigating to eBay. They can type the URL of eBay's home page, **www.ebay.com**, into a web browser's address bar (1). However, a quicker way for users not accustomed to using the URL address bar might be to type in the word *ebay* into search box on the Google home page (2), or to type *ebay.com* into the Google search box within the web browser (3).

FIGURE 2.14 Searchers have some options to get to eBay's home page. If a searcher uses a commercial web search engine to navigate to a site, the query is a navigational query, and the keywords used to arrive at the web page are navigational keywords.

Transactional Queries

Many search engine marketers tend to spend a great deal of time focusing on transactional queries because they want to target searchers who are ready to buy. On the surface, focusing on a specific point in the buying cycle might seem like a great way to save time and money. However, this strategy may cost website owners prospects and lifetime customers.

Informational Queries

Before people make a buying decision, they often begin a web search session with an informational query to establish a frame of reference: Which companies offer the products? How much do these products generally cost? Can shoppers get these products only online, or can they quickly drive to a nearby physical location to purchase this product? If there is a nearby (offline) physical store, how can they get there?

■ CONCLUSION

Key points in this chapter:

- Savvy marketers should understand *how* people are searching and *why* people are searching in order to formulate the best search engine marketing strategies.

- When people use the commercial web search engines, they are trying to communicate where they want to go (navigational), what they want to read (informational), and what they want to do (transactional).

- By increasing the scent of information in search listings, site owners can encourage users to click their listings and maintain their site's search engine visibility, meeting both user expectations and business objectives.

- In web search, the scent of information consists of the keywords that people type into search engines.

- Search engine optimization professionals view querying as a positive search behavior.

- Usability professionals sometimes view querying as a negative search behavior because it can indicate a missing scent of information.

- Web searchers want their information scents validated in search engine results pages (SERPs). Web search engines, such as Google, get the information to display in search listings from your web pages' content.

- Every portion of a search listing—title tag, meta-tag content or page snippet, and URL—is important for the scent of information, user confidence, and clickability.

- Web search queries are classified based on searcher intent: navigational (where can I go?), informational (what can I read or learn?), and transactional (what can I do?).

- By satisfying navigational, informational, and transactional query needs, website owners can get a higher ROI than by satisfying transactional queries alone.

CHAPTER 3

NAVIGATIONAL SEARCHES— WHERE CAN I GO?

With a navigational query, a web searcher's main goal is to go directly to a website's home page or to a specific website page. The term *navigational query* refers to people using commercial web search engines to go (navigate) to a specific website page.

Navigational queries are important to site owners because searchers who perform them genuinely wish to visit your site. Web searchers might want to visit your site to find specific information (such as your company's or organization's phone number) or to perform a transaction (buy, enroll, log in, and so forth). Regardless of the searcher's final goal, many query sessions begin with navigational intent.

Navigational queries are more common than you might imagine, comprising between 10 percent and 26 percent of web search engine queries. Clearly, a considerable number of web searchers want to go to specific websites. Let's look at how to determine that a search is navigational and how to ensure your site meets searchers' expectations.

■ NAVIGATIONAL INTENT

Searchers formulate navigational queries because they might not know or remember the URL of the site. They might type the abbreviation of a company's name because the official company name is long and easily misspelled. Searchers might only remember part of a URL. Or searchers might simply find it easier to type in the company name in a search box rather than an organization's full URL in the address bar of a web browser (**Figure 3.1**). This occurs more frequently than you might imagine.

FIGURE 3.1 During usability tests, you often see users typing the word "Google" to arrive at Google's home page from Yahoo!, and vice versa. When we ask usability test participants why they use a Yahoo! search to go to Google's home page, they usually say that it is easier to just type in a single keyword rather than the full URL. Interestingly, many searchers are not even aware that they can type in a URL in a browser's address bar.

Typically, navigational queries occur more frequently on mobile phones and PDAs (personal digital assistants). These devices have much smaller screens than desktop and laptop computers. Therefore, searchers have less space to type in keywords, and less space to view corresponding search results. PDAs and mobile phones also have smaller keyboards. Therefore, searchers tend to type in fewer keywords with fewer characters when they use a mobile search engine.

Additionally, the address bar is not always easily recognizable on a mobile device. Many searchers do not even know where to type a known web address. So they type in all or part of a URL in an area of the screen that is familiar to them—the search field (**Figure 3.2**). In a recent studies, 17 percent of English-language Google mobile queries were for URLs; Microsoft reported a smaller percentage (7.54 percent); Yahoo! reported an even smaller one (5 percent). For this and more information about querying research, see "A Large Scale Study of Wireless Search Behavior: Google Mobile Search" by Kumvar and Baluja at http://www1.cs.columbia.edu/~mkamvar/publications/CHI_06.pdf; "On Mobile User Behaviour Patterns" by Milan Vojnovic at http://research.microsoft.com/apps/pubs/default.aspx?id=70532; and "Deciphering Mobile Search Patterns: A Study of Yahoo! Mobile Search Queries" by Yi et al at http://www2008.org/papers/pdf/fp846-yi.pdf.

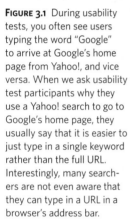

FIGURE 3.2 In this Apple iPhone figure, the searcher is using the default search engine (Google) instead of the unlabeled address bar to go to eBay's home page.

Web search engine companies usability test continually to improve the searcher experience. To determine whether people are using web search to navigate, search engines analyze keyword combinations and corresponding clicks; which search listings users click on most frequently; and whether the search session ends once users arrive at destination sites.

If the word combinations or characters clearly indicate navigational intent, search engines tend to place specific listings in positions one through three of the search engine results page (SERP). Searchers rarely look past the first two or three listings for queries with navigational intent. Let's take a look at some examples of navigational queries.

Example 1: Home Pages

Suppose a searcher wants to go to the National Cancer Institute's home page. Instead of typing in the words **National Cancer Institute** in Google, she types in the abbreviation for the organization (**NCI**) because it is easier and faster to type than the full name. She also types in the top-level domain extension **.gov** because she remembers that the National Cancer Institute is a government website.

She uses Google search instead of the address bar because Google is her computer's default home page, and, in the past, she successfully arrived at the National Cancer Institute's website using this search strategy. **Figure 3.3** shows Google's search engine results page from this query.

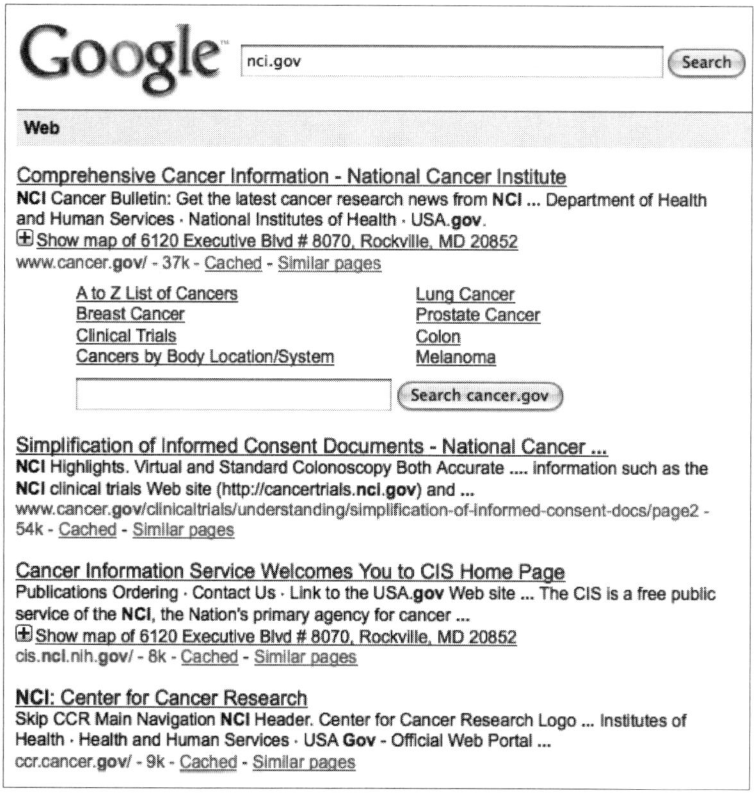

NOTE Currently, search engines do not use the number of clicks (click popularity) to determine search engine rankings, except in the area of *personalized search*. With personalized search, search engines are able to tailor search listings for each user based on past search history, which sites the user clicks on most often, bookmarks, and other factors. The data from personalized search can help search engines determine whether a searcher's intent is navigational, informational, or transactional.

FIGURE 3.3 Because the searcher typed in an abbreviation and a domain extension in the search box, Google determined that the searcher's intent was most likely to be navigational.

The query entry communicates strong navigational intent. In all likelihood, the searcher probably wants to go to a government website (.gov) with the abbreviation NCI. The National Cancer Institute's canonical domain name is cancer.gov, and Google correctly forwarded the searcher to the appropriate website's home page URL.

Query entries are considered to be URLs if they begin with http or www, or if they contain *.com, .org, .edu, .net,* or any other common top-level domain (TLD) extension.

What if a searcher only remembered part of the organization's name but still wanted to go to that specific website? A searcher might type in part of the organization's name, as shown in **Figure 3.4**:

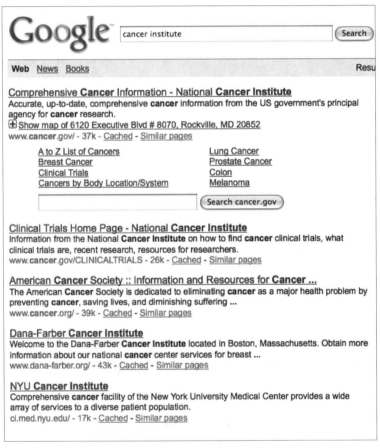

FIGURE 3.4 Since the searcher did not remember whether the official organization name was the National Cancer Institute or the American Cancer Institute, she typed in the part of the name that she remembered, hoping that Google would deliver search results that would lead her to the right website.

CANONICAL DOMAIN NAMES

A *canonical domain name* is the standard, or authoritative, domain name that you wish site visitors to see. A canonical domain should be reduced to the simplest and most vital form possible without being overly general.

For example, searchers can go to the National Cancer Institute's home page via the following URLs:

- http://www.cancer.gov
- http://www.nci.gov
- http://nci.nih.gov

In Figures 3.3 and 3.4, Google has selected the URL www.cancer.gov as the most appropriate URL for the National Cancer Institute's home page. For more information about canonicalization, visit www.mattcutts.com/blog/seo-advice-url-canonicalization/.

To accommodate searchers who have navigational intent, site owners should be proactive and purchase multiple domain names, not only for their official company name but also for abbreviations of their company name, established brands, and trademarked terms. Consider purchasing domain names with common misspellings of any of these domains. Some unscrupulous web marketers count on domain misspellings to trap unwary users.

Example 2: Login Pages

One of the most interesting aspects of website usability is differentiating what people *say* from what people *do*. During usability tests, usability professionals encourage test participants to think out loud to help them determine why participants make specific choices on a web page, such as which links to click on. Usability professionals also measure and observe actual user behavior. All too often, people say they are going to do something (click on a link) but then perform an action that you might not expect.

In the web search industry, users saying one thing and doing another happens quite frequently. Look at **Figure 3.5**. What type of keywords do you believe this searcher will generate? Do you believe the keywords will be navigational, informational, or transactional?

On the surface, the searcher's intent is both informational (because he wants to see how many frequent flyer miles he has accumulated) and transactional (because he will probably have

FIGURE 3.5 What is this user's intent? Navigational, informational, or transactional?

to log in to his account in order to acquire this information). However, this particular searcher generated the following query and was given these search results (**Figure 3.6**):

FIGURE 3.6 What the searcher said and what the searcher did were quite different.

NOTE Details for keyword research can be found in Part 2 of *Search Engine Visibility*, 2nd Edition, by Shari Thurow (New Riders Publishing, 2007).

Even though the searcher stated that he wanted to check his frequent flyer miles, his web search query was only one word, *united*. Before the searcher could check the number of miles he has accumulated, and before he could log in to his account, he had to first go to the website where he could log in (in this case, the United Airlines website). He used a web search engine to navigate to a specific site. Single-word queries might be navigational if the organization's brand is very well known. In fact, one- or two-word queries are a strong indication of navigational intent.

Search engine marketing (SEM) professionals regularly research keyword phrases to determine searchers' intent. Keyword research tools (available online) help SEM professionals determine how people search and the approximate volume of keywords used per month. Data from web analytics software and site search engines can also show how searchers are formulating queries.

However, SEM professionals must look beyond this data and look at the big picture. In this example, if SEM professionals only focused on how many times per month people searched for the word *united*, they would not understand *why* searchers formulate that query. They might assume that the searchers' only goal was to go to the United Airlines home page.

■ LEARN THE KEYWORDS IN YOUR USERS' MENTAL MODELS

During usability testing, ask test participants the simple question, "How would you look for this information on the web?" Their answers and actions will often reveal their intentions and the steps to complete their desired tasks. You can see query formulation firsthand if they use the web search engines to complete tasks. You can also witness frustration with terminology and labeling within search listings and corresponding landing pages. Does the content of landing pages match the searchers' mental models?

Keyword data alone does not reveal searchers' underlying motivations for formulating search queries. Keyword data, combined with usability test data, can reveal searchers' motivations.

Example 3: Category and Channel Pages

Sometimes searchers want to navigate to a specific page within a specific website. They do not want to go to the home page and browse the site to find desired information, especially if their desired information is buried deep within a site's information architecture. They want to go directly to the "right" page. Sometimes, the "right" page is a category or a channel page.

> **NOTE** A *channel page* is a top-level category page. Sometimes, a channel page is referred to as a *department page*. To illustrate, the vertical hierarchy of a website might look like: Home > Channel > Category > Subcategory > Content.

For example, let's use the Apple website. Searchers might want to go to Apple's website for a variety of reasons. They might want to buy something, download some music, or get technical support.

Suppose a searcher wants to see the variety of iPods that are available before deciding to buy one. He might want to see the cool stuff he can download on the different types of iPods before purchasing. He periodically might visit the Apple website because he knows he can download cool stuff directly from the site. In other words, this searcher could very easily become a repeat visitor and lifetime customer.

To find the content on the web, the searcher might type in the keyword phrase **apple ipod** into Google and get the search results shown in **Figure 3.7**:

FIGURE 3.7 Google SERP for the query words *apple ipod*.

Google tried to deliver the most appropriate web listings based on these query words. Google has interpreted that the searcher wishes to see information about iPods on Apple's official website. A channel page (iPod + iTunes) is the top search listing.

By using the keyword "apple" as part of the search query, the searcher might be communicating that he wishes to view desired content on Apple's official website. In Google's main search results in Figure 3.7 you see that Google has accommodated a navigational query for *Apple ipod* in the number 1 and number 2 positions, presenting a channel page in position 1, and a category page in position 2. **Figure 3.8** shows the landing page for the listing in the number 1 position.

FIGURE 3.8 Landing page after clicking the top search listing link shown in Figure 3.7, the iPod + iTunes channel page.

Since navigational queries can lead to transactions (downloads, purchases, and so on), search engine marketing professionals should test transactional querying by purchasing advertisements for some navigational query words.

If the searcher wants to see a list of available iPods, this is a very appropriate landing page. The searcher can easily view the variety of available iPod types (iPod shuffle, iPod nano, iPod classic, iPod touch) immediately at the top of the screen. Each graphic image is labeled with appropriate text. The folks at Apple have optimized this channel page quite effectively for this type of search query. The highlighted navigation button at the top of the screen communicates that visitors are in the iPod + iTunes section. The available iPods are shown right away at the top of the screen, and the page identifiers (title tags, page content, headings, URL or web address) communicate it as well. The "you are here" cues, which provide a sense of place, and the information scents are very clear.

Since navigational queries can lead to transactions (downloads, purchases, and so on), search engine marketing professionals should test transactional querying by purchasing advertisements for some navigational query words. Notice that in the search results page shown in Figure 3.7, Apple has purchased advertising space for a particular type of iPod. If searchers click on that advertisement, they are not delivered to the same landing page shown in Figure 3.8. Instead, they are delivered to a specific page that accommodates transactional intent. This is clear on the landing page because pricing is available on this advertisement's landing page (**Figure 3.9**) that is not available on the channel page.

FIGURE 3.9 A searcher who is ready to make a purchase will want to see specific prices or a price range.

■ SEARCH LISTINGS AND NAVIGATIONAL QUERIES

The goal of commercial web search engines is to deliver searchers to their desired content as quickly and as easily as possible. Likewise, searchers' main desire is to leave a web search engine to arrive at their desired website (or web page) as quickly as possible. With navigational queries, searchers do not have the patience to explore search results. In their eyes, a query with navigational intent has a clear, right answer.

Searchers who perform navigational queries rarely look past the first three positions, and they are not paying much attention to the snippets in each search listing. Instead, they focus their attention on the link, which is taken from a web page's title tag, and the URL as shown in **Figure 3.10**:

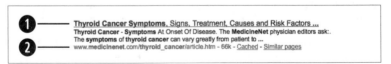

FIGURE 3.10 For a navigational query, the two most important items in a search listing are (1) the title-tag content, and (2) the URL.

Once searchers determine that the web address is the right one, they click on the hypertext link in the search listing. They do not return to the search engine but rather stay on the site they wished to navigate to.

The URL is very important for navigational queries. If a URL is too long, searchers tend to look past it for listings with shorter URLs. For example, let's compare the following URLs.

- www.companyname.com/New_York_City/New_York_City-Restaurants/New_York_City-Restaurants-Thai/Thai-Restaurants.html (113 characters)

- www.companyname.com/New-York-City/Restaurants/thai.html (56 characters)

Even if the first URL were in the number 1 position, searchers would focus their attention on the listing in the number 2 position. So it is best to keep URLs as short and descriptive as possible. For navigational queries, a good rule of thumb is to keep URL length to less than 65 characters, if possible.

Remember that some people who type in navigational keywords are likely to be repeat visitors. In fact, a recent study from Google U.K. and comScore revealed that online travel buyers change the type of keywords as they move along the path to purchase. Of all the consumers sampled who made a final purchase, 29 percent started with a non-branded keyword phrase but ended with a branded keyword phrase. The branded keyword phrase was likely an indication of navigational intent. Web searchers want to go back to sites they have previously visited.

Google accommodates navigational queries differently for U.K.–based search listings and U.S.–based search listings. Soccer is not nearly as popular in the U.S. as it is in the U.K. It is unlikely that U.S.–based searchers who use the keyword *united* want to go to the Manchester United website (**Figure 3.11** on the next page). However, in other areas of the world, this site is exactly where searchers wish to go (**Figure 3.12** on the next page). Notice how Google is keeping the top positions in the U.K.–based search results to accommodate a keyword with navigational intent.

If the Manchester United site owners want search engine visibility at the top of Google U.S. search listings, they could purchase Google ads for this keyword, to appear specifically on Google U.S. search results. If the return on investment (ROI) for this navigational keyword is high, then it is worth it for them to maintain the ad as long as it continues to deliver ROI. However, if the commercial web search engines are delivering the site's home page for navigational searches, it might not be necessary to purchase advertising for the organization name, thus saving search advertising expenses.

NOTE See *Marketing-Sherpa's Search Marketing Guide 2008* for more details about URL length.

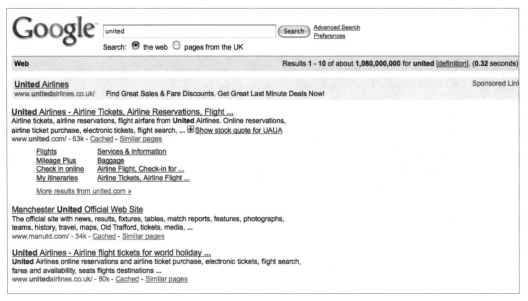

Figure 3.11 Google U.K. (United Kingdom) search results.

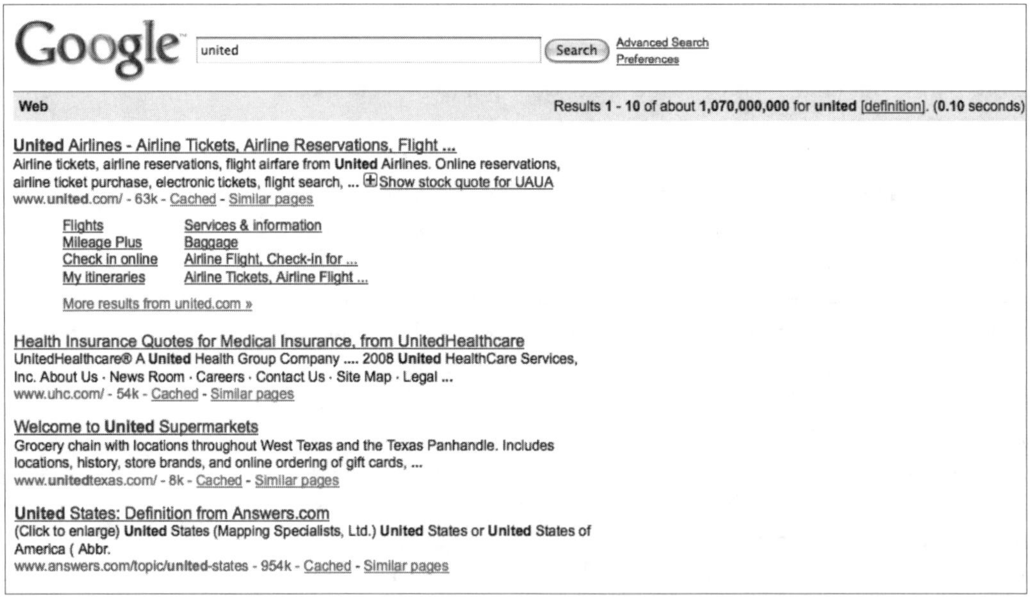

Figure 3.12 Google U.S. search results. Notice that the Manchester United website is not listed in the top three positions.

■ NAVIGATIONAL QUERY INDICATORS

Your web analytics data can help you determine which keywords show navigational intent. Some navigational query indicators include:

- Portions of URLs (such as http and www)
- Common domain suffixes (*.com, .org, .edu, .net,* and so forth)
- Company, business, and brand names
- Keyword phrases comprised of one or two words

NOTE At the beginning of 2008, Google announced that the average number of words per query has increased to four words per query.

■ OPTIMIZING FOR NAVIGATIONAL QUERIES

Here are some general guidelines for optimizing your website to accommodate navigational queries:

- Make it easy for the search engines to put your site's home page in top positions for your company name. Your site's home page and "About Us" pages should be optimized for your company's official name. Optimize more than just your home page for informational and transactional keywords.
- The URL is very important for navigational queries. Keep URL length to less than 65 characters, whenever possible, for pages that typically satisfy searchers' navigational intent.
- For pages that you know will be important for navigational intent, keep the meta-tag description short for easy reading, but descriptive and explanatory (**Figure 3.13**).

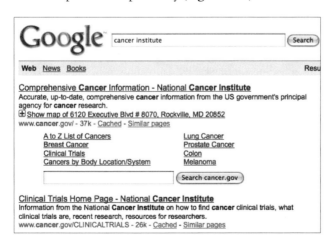

FIGURES 3.13 The National Cancer Institute did an outstanding job of writing a short meta-tag description for its home page, around 105 characters.

- Be realistic about search engine positioning. If you periodically monitor how search listings appear for your targeted keyword phrases, you will learn which websites and individual web pages stay in the top positions for navigational queries. It might be unrealistic to expect your listing to be in the first position if it does not clearly meet searchers' navigational intent.

- Buy domains that have your brands, company name, and trademarks in them. If it is not possible due to budgetary limitations, then at least put those items in other places in a URL using the "URL Structure (Web Address)" section in Chapter 2, "The Scent of Information and Web Search Engines," as a guideline.

■ CONCLUSION

Key points in this chapter:

- Navigational queries are important to website owners because searchers who perform them genuinely wish to visit your site.

- When a searcher types in all or portions of a URL as a keyword, it is a strong indication that the searcher's intent is navigational.

- To accommodate searchers who have navigational intent, site owners should be proactive and purchase domain names for their official organization or company name, abbreviations of their company name, established brands, and trademarked terms.

- If your organization does not have an easily recognized name or abbreviation, then ensure the most appropriate ads and corresponding landing pages appear for company-name searches. Apple does an outstanding job at appropriate page delivery.

- The URL structure (web address) in a search listing is very important for searchers who wish to go to a specific website.

- Keep URL length to less than 65 characters, whenever possible, for pages that typically satisfy searchers' navigational intent.

- In the event that the commercial web search engines are delivering your site's home page for navigational searches, it might not be necessary to purchase advertising for your company name, thus saving search advertising expenses.

- The description or snippet is not as important as the URL structure for navigational searches. Keep the meta-tag description short (around 100 to 150 characters) for pages that typically satisfy searchers' navigational intent.

CHAPTER 4

INFORMATIONAL SEARCHES— WHAT CAN I LEARN?

An informational query is one in which the searcher's goal is obtaining information about a general or specific topic. Sometimes a searcher wants quick information, such as how to do something. And sometimes a searcher wants to delve deeper into a topic, and is willing to do considerable research before making a business transaction.

Informational queries are the most common type of web search query, comprising between 48 percent and 80 percent of web searches. What do these numbers mean to website owners? If a site owner wants to get and maintain long-term search engine visibility, then satisfying informational searches is crucial. All websites should contain informational pages that provide specific content of user interest. Let's look at how to determine that a search is informational and how to ensure your site meets searchers' expectations.

■ INFORMATIONAL INTENT

Many web search sessions begin with an informational query and end with a transaction. People will not purchase your products and services if you do not provide them with enough content to make an informed decision, especially for high-ticket items.

For example, on an ecommerce site, searchers might be interested in locating something in the real world (such as a physical location of a store), or they might be interested in seeing a list of available items. Many product or shopping queries have a "locate" goal because online shoppers want to know where they can purchase a desired product. In fact, the plural form of a targeted keyword can be a strong indication that searchers wish to view a list of available products.

Category pages are a type of information page because they contain lists of available items. **Figure 4.1** shows a standard format for a category page. Another category page format is an annotated list. The annotated list format can provide a stronger information scent because the annotation text can contain additional keywords as well, reinforcing existing keywords on the page (**Figure 4.2**).

FIGURE 4.1 A category page is a type of information page because it contains a list of products that searchers might wish to view and compare before making a purchase. For high-ticket items such as furniture, cars, and plane tickets, searchers typically visit many websites to gather information before buying.

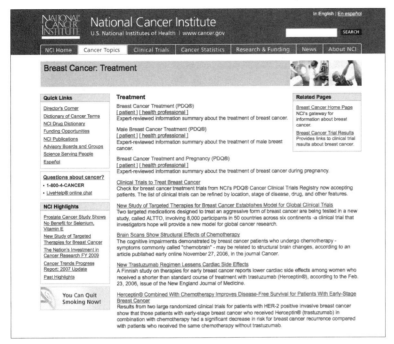

FIGURE 4.2 A topical category page on the National Cancer Institute website. The annotated list format provides many opportunities for keyword placement.

Proper keyword selection and placement can make an annotated category page appear more topically focused to both searchers and search engines. In other words, the page format shown in Figure 4.2 is an effective format for people who query *and* for people who browse.

Let's take a look at some more examples of informational queries.

Example 1: Quick Facts

Search sessions can be long or short when a searcher wants information about a topic. Of course, if searchers want a quick fact, they prefer to make the search session as short as possible.

In **Figure 4.3** on the next page, our searcher is traveling to London and wants to see what the weather is like. Notice that the top three search listings are not official company sites. Even Weather.com's listing is not in the top three results, meaning that the search engine has determined that the keyword phrase (*weather in London*) does not indicate a navigational goal. It is most likely an informational goal. The searcher is using Google to find out about the current London weather, not to navigate to a specific website.

FIGURE 4.3 A search engine results page for an informational query. Notice that the top positions are not dedicated to navigational queries. These search listings strongly indicate that this keyword phrase shows informational intent.

Searchers do not always show informational intent with their keyword selection. For example, in **Figure 4.4**, what type of keywords do you believe this searcher, a Manchester United soccer team fan located in England, will generate? Do you believe the keywords will be navigational, informational, or transactional?

On the surface, the searcher's intent appears to be informational. He can view the match schedule on multiple websites. He does not have to go to the official Manchester United website to view the match schedule.

However, this particular searcher typed the word *united* in Google and received the search results in **Figure 4.5**:

FIGURE 4.4 Is this searcher's intent navigational, informational, or transactional?

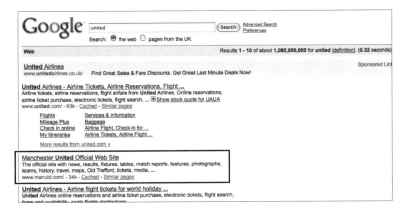

FIGURE 4.5 What the Manchester United fan said and what he did were quite different.

Even though the searcher stated that he wanted to see the match schedule, his web search query was for only one word, *united*. His actions did not match his words. He clearly wanted to go to the official Manchester United website to view the match schedule.

> *Field studies and exploratory usability tests often reveal searchers' informational goals above and beyond what can be inferred from web analytics data and keyword research tools.*

Moral of the story? To see such discrepancy between words and actions, it is very important to have some one-on-one, face-to-face contact with searchers. Observe what users do as well as what they say. Web analytics data will only show that this type of searcher wants to go to the official Manchester United website. The data does not show this searcher's informational goal. Field studies and exploratory usability tests often reveal searchers' informational goals above and beyond what can be inferred from web analytics data and keyword research tools.

Example 2: Questions and Answers

One of the strongest indicators of informational intent is a keyword phrase that is formatted as a question, such as:

- How do I get driving directions to your office?
- Where are the nearest parking garages near this restaurant [name]?
- What is the capital of Nigeria?
- What are your hours of operation?
- What does the abbreviation NMR mean?

Question-formatted keyword phrases present a great opportunity for multiple types of search engine optimization, particularly how-to keyword phrases. Searchers might want to see graphic image instructions and diagrams that they can eventually print. Searchers might also want to watch a video that shows them how to do a procedure. One way to see how search engines determine the best results for question-and-answer queries is to monitor search engine results pages to see what types of listings appear on the first few pages (**Figure 4.6**).

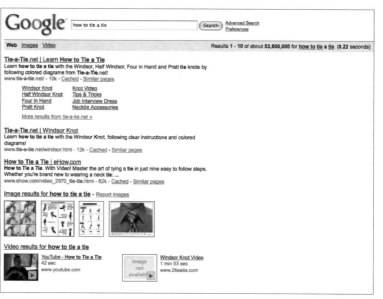

Note You can find details for graphic image and video optimization in Part 3 of *Search Engine Visibility,* 2nd Edition, by Shari Thurow (New Riders Publishing, 2007).

Figure 4.6 For many informational searches, there are multiple ways that your listing can appear on the first page of search results. Like web page listings, graphic image files and video files should be optimized in order for them to appear in the top search results. How-to files present a great opportunity to satisfy informational queries.

A natural place to implement keyword phrases in a question-answer format is a Frequently Asked Questions (FAQs) section of a website. However, some usability professionals do not recommend having an FAQs section. They say that most users should be able to have all their informational needs addressed on main content pages and category pages, making the FAQs section unnecessary.

Nevertheless, users have questions about products, services, delivery options, hours of operation, guarantees, and so on. And users often format their search queries as questions. Can you imagine formatting a product page on an ecommerce site in a question-answer, question-answer format? That format would probably confuse users. And a question-answer format isn't really an appropriate format for a product page. However, an FAQs section of a website is a legitimate and accepted way to satisfy question-formatted informational queries.

In addition, a customer service or FAQs section is often more flexible than other sections of a website. If your customer service staff, or others who have direct one-on-one contact with your users, determines that customers and prospects keep asking the same question over and over again, adding that question to an FAQs page is an easy process.

> **TIP** Other names for question-answer pages include *Help* and *Customer Service*. If your target audience is likely to not understand the *FAQs* abbreviation for *Frequently Asked Questions*, use *Help* or *Customer Service* as an alternative navigation label.

Example 3: Lists

When searchers wish to delve deeper into a topic of interest, they often type keyword phrases that they hope will provide them with a list of suggestions and a frame of reference for further research. Sites that provide a topical list of resources, particularly annotated lists that easily validate an information scent, often appear at the top of search engine listings (**Figure 4.7**). Sections of a website that typically give a topical list of resources include Links, Resources, and Tips sections.

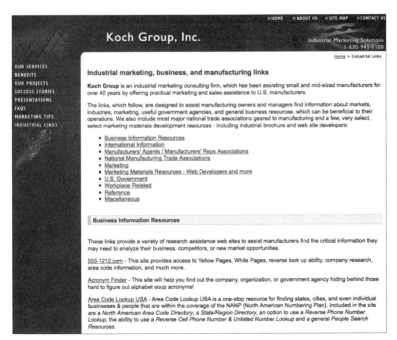

FIGURE 4.7 An annotated links page on a business-to-business (B2B) website. Notice that the page is a long one, and the site owners have clearly indicated that content is available below the fold via the bulleted hypertext links. The scent of information is maintained above the fold as well as below the fold. In addition, the repetition of important keywords helps with search engine visibility.

> **NOTE** On a web page, *above the fold* refers to content that is located near the top of the page, content that can be viewed in a browser without scrolling.

TIP An important tip that warrants repeating about many category pages from a search usability perspective: The plural form of a query word should naturally occur on this type of page within the title tag, heading, locational breadcrumb links, and introductory paragraph (if used).

Another type of web page that naturally contains a list is a category page, as illustrated at the beginning of this chapter in Figures 4.1 and 4.2. One thing to remember about many category pages from a search usability perspective: The plural form of a query word should naturally occur on this type of page within the title tag, heading, locational breadcrumb links, and introductory paragraph (if used).

Individual product pages should emphasize the singular form of a word, with a few exceptions. One exception: If a product page contains links to other product pages containing the same word, providing a strong scent of information, then searchers find it acceptable to see both the singular and plural form of a word on a page (**Figure 4.8**).

FIGURE 4.8 This product page links to other product pages containing the word *saw*.

Another exception is a product page that offers a set of items, such as a set of tools. In this instance, the plural form of a word is a natural occurrence. However, a product page that emphasizes a set of items does not necessarily provide a good frame of reference for further research. Therefore, a product page for a *set* of items will not likely rank well for informational queries where searchers want a *list* of items.

■ SEARCH LISTINGS AND INFORMATIONAL QUERIES

Search engine results pages communicate a lot of information in individual search listings, including what search engines determine to be searcher intent. For example, suppose a searcher wishes to buy a refrigerator, a high-ticket item. Before going to the store and purchasing a refrigerator, he wishes to see the types of fridges available since he has not had to purchase a fridge for a very long time. To establish a frame of reference, he only types in a single keyword, *refrigerators*, as shown in **Figure 4.9**:

FIGURE 4.9 Search engine results page for the query word *refrigerators*.

What might the arrangement and placement of these search listings communicate to us? First, we see a wide variety of listing types supporting varied intentions among various searchers. In the search listings are:

- Product review pages
- A government website
- Category pages
- Shopping search listings
- Wikipedia

Whenever you see a Wikipedia listing appear on the first page of web search results, it is a strong indication that the search engine has determined that the keyword (or keyword phrase) is an informational query. Wikipedia is an informational website. In contrast, online retail sites are primarily transactional sites.

By focusing only on transactional queries and ignoring informational queries, many site owners are probably losing initial sales and potential lifetime customers.

Therefore, whenever a website owner sees a Wikipedia listing appear in search results, she should immediately think, "Are there pages on my website that meet searchers' informational needs?" If not, then it is unrealistic to expect pages from your site to appear at the top of search results for that query type. Adding appropriate product reviews, how-to tips, and maybe an FAQs section can help your site appear in web search results for informational query words.

By focusing only on transactional queries and ignoring informational queries, many site owners are probably losing initial sales and potential lifetime customers. Wikipedia listings can actually help remind site owners to build more effective information into their sites. Retailer listings can peacefully coexist with Wikipedia listings. No one ever lost a sale to Wikipedia.

In web search results, the listing title and description/snippet are the most important elements for searchers with informational goals. Informational searchers want to be sure that they are clicking a link that delivers them to desired content. So they take the extra time to read the listing description/snippet (**Figure 4.10**). The URL becomes less important to searchers because the desired information, not necessarily the URL, is the main target.

FIGURE 4.10 For an informational query, the two most important items in a search listing are (1) the title-tag content, and (2) the page snippet or meta-tag description.

On one hand, many major search engines use the meta-tag description when displaying a page's (or file's) listing. The content in the meta-tag description should accomplish the following:

- Encourage searchers to click the link to your web page.
- Reinforce content that is already available (and visible to users) on the page, and as a result provides and validates the scent of information.
- Help to obtain top positions in the search results for search engines that use meta-tag descriptions to determine rankings.

On the other hand, search engines do not always take listing descriptions from meta-tag descriptions. Search engines might take the listing description from other on-the-page content, or use a combination of the two. For this reason, meta-tag content should reinforce the most important keyword phrases description already available on a web page.

■ INFORMATIONAL QUERY INDICATORS

Your web analytics data and keyword research data can help you determine which query words show informational intent. Some informational query indicators include:

- Question words (*how, what, where, why, who, when*)
- Keyword phrases with four or more words per phrase
- Plural form of a word (indicating the desire to see a list of items for further research)

Search engine results pages also provide strong indicators of informational intent. If you see Wikipedia consistently appear in search results for many of your targeted keyword phrases, search engines have determined that searchers who type in those keyword phrases want to read information about that topic. Likewise, if you see other types of informational websites (reference, how-to, and so on) dominate the top search results, then search engines have deemed those keyword combinations as informational.

■ OPTIMIZING FOR INFORMATIONAL QUERIES

Here are some general guidelines for optimizing your website to accommodate informational queries:

- For pages that you know will be important for searchers' informational queries, spend the extra time to write longer (200–250 characters) meta-tag descriptions.

- Do not use the same meta-tag descriptions across an entire site. Write unique meta-tag content for each web page, especially pages that are likely to appear at the top of web search results for informational queries. Category pages, how-to pages, and annotated links/resources pages are types of information pages.

- Since search engines do not always use a meta-tag description as the search listing's description, make sure that other page content (headings, paragraphs, bulleted lists, and so on) contains important keywords. The double exposure of keywords in meta-tag descriptions and keywords in the main content area gets the best long-term results.

- The plural form of a word can be a strong indication that searchers desire to view a list of products and/or services. Many category and channel pages should be optimized for the plural form of a targeted keyword.

- Do not ignore other types of optimization strategies for informational queries. Images and videos are also desirable responses to informational queries. Graphic images and videos should be optimized as well as the text-based pages that contain them. Local search listings can provide quick information as well, such as hours of operation, location, and telephone number(s).

Even if searchers do not initially click your informational search listing, they do notice when your site keeps appearing over and over again for topically related keyword phrases. After seeing your site appear for a wide variety of keyword phrases, user confidence in your brand tends to increase. Remember, though, user confidence can plummet with one click if the scent of information is not validated quickly. Users remember the sites that did not deliver, and they will not click future listings.

■ CONCLUSION

Key points in this chapter:

■ Informational queries are important to website owners because they are the most common type of search engine query. Satisfying informational searches is crucial for a site's long-term search engine visibility.

■ Many web search sessions begin with an informational query and end with a transaction.

■ All websites should contain informational pages. They provide specific content of user interest.

■ Some types of informational pages include category pages, channel pages, FAQs or customer service pages, and pages that contain topical lists of resources (such as Links, Resources, and Tips sections).

■ Field studies and exploratory usability tests often reveal searchers' informational goals above and beyond what can be inferred from web analytics data and keyword research tools.

■ Longer keyword phrases (more than three words) tend to be informational queries; shorter ones tend to be navigational queries.

■ If question words (*how, what, where, why, who, when*) are part of a keyword phrase, then the keyword phrase is an informational query.

■ The plural form of a word can be a strong indication that searchers desire to view a list of products. Many category and channel pages should be optimized for the plural form of a targeted keyword.

■ The appearance of Wikipedia and other how-to listings in search results is a strong indication that the query words show informational intent by the users.

■ The description or snippet is more important than the URL structure for informational searches. Keep the meta-tag description longer (around 200 to 250 characters) for pages that typically satisfy searchers informational intent.

■ Do not use the same meta-tag description on every page of a site. Tailor meta-tag descriptions to reflect actual page content.

CHAPTER 5

TRANSACTIONAL SEARCHES—WHAT CAN I DO?

With a transactional query, a searcher's main goal is to perform some sort of activity beyond merely reading. Sometimes the activity occurs online, such as downloading software, watching a video, or playing an online game. And sometimes the activity ultimately will occur offline, such as purchasing bedroom furniture or going to the dentist. Approximately 10 to 24 percent of web queries are transactional.

Transactional queries are important to website owners and search engine optimization professionals because they both hope to capture searchers at a critical point in the buying process: right when they are ready to buy and provide personal information (such as name, address, phone number, email address, and so on). Let's look at how to determine that a search is transactional and how to ensure your site meets searchers' expectations.

Additionally, items such as videos, sound files, slide shows, games, and so forth can increase the stickiness of a site, encouraging site visitors to stay on your site longer and view more content. Popular and informative interactive items can also increase a site's external, third-party link development, which has a direct impact on a website's rankings.

■ TRANSACTIONAL INTENT

Determining transactional intent can be tricky because searchers do not always type the activity they wish to perform as a keyword. For example, a person might be interested in buying some crystal water goblets but does not type in the word *buy* or *purchase* as query words (**Figure 5.1**).

FIGURE 5.1 A searcher who wishes to buy some water goblets will probably not type the word *buy* in the search box. Yet this searcher might be ready to buy. Notice that Google has placed shopping search results at the top of this search results page, accommodating searchers with transactional intent.

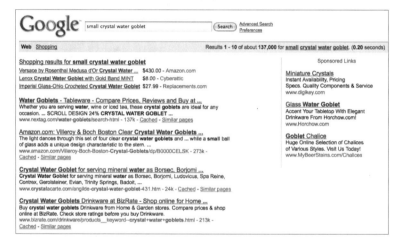

As another example, searchers might want to enroll in a class or watch a video but not type the word *enroll* or *watch* as part of the search query. They might want to listen to the latest song by their favorite band but not type the word *listen* as part of the search query. They might want to play a game of Sudoku but not type the word *play*. Searchers can show transactional intent by using nouns (*video*, *music*, *game*) as well as verbs (*download*, *chat*, *enroll*). The activity might occur on an actual website, such as getting a quote for auto insurance. Or the activity might occur offline, such as making a phone call to a local pharmacy to refill a prescription. For product-oriented nouns, consider that users might have both informational and transactional intent.

Nevertheless, an easier case occurs when searchers do type the exact activity they wish to perform. The words *download*, *apply*, *search*, and *find* are more commonly used than you might imagine. Regular keyword research often reveals the precise action that searchers wish to take, and these action words (usually verbs) should appear in search listings as well as corresponding landing pages. Web pages that satisfy transactional intent do have special features, as shown in the following examples.

Example 1: Buying Products

Product pages on an ecommerce site should satisfy transactional queries. Since searchers with transactional intent wish to perform a specific activity, product pages that meet their expectations should include the following items:

- Actual query words (to validate the scent of information)
- Words associated with the desired activity (such as *Add to Cart*, associated with the words *buy* or *purchase*)
- Clear call to action
- Enough graphic and textual information (such as a product photo, product description, and price) to close the sale

All of this information should appear above the fold, so that site visitors do not have to scroll. In other words, searchers' most desired information *and* desired transactional keywords should appear above the fold. **Figure 5.2** shows portions of a product page that meet the expectations of online shoppers with transactional intent. As an added bonus, such pages satisfy users' informational intent as well.

FIGURE 5.2 Searchers' most desired information appears above the fold: product name, short product description, price, and the primary call to action (Add to Cart).

A category page can also meet the needs and expectations of online shoppers with clear transactional intent. Product names, prices, thumbnail photos, and clear calls to action are normally portions of an ecommerce site's category page (**Figure 5.3**).

FIGURE 5.3 Category pages can also meet searchers' transactional expectations.

Category pages often appear in web search results for transactional queries, although searchers prefer to view more detailed product pages before making a final purchasing decision, especially for high-ticket items. Product pages provide more screen real estate for keyword placement, too.

Example 2: Entertainment

Transactional intent does not automatically mean the desire to purchase a product or service. People also use the web for entertainment. Recent years have seen a global explosion in online video viewing, photo sharing, and audio file downloads.

However, Flash videos and splash pages in search results can cause searcher frustration. Here are a few reasons that many users dislike Flash videos:

- Delays the scent of information (users have to watch a video before they see their keywords validated)

- Diminishes the scent of information (videos tend not to be keyword focused)

- Hides the scent of information (site visitors never see their keywords validated on a web page)

After users click a link to a web page from a search engine listing, they generally do not want to watch a video (which might be an advertisement) before they see their user-generated information scent validated. They become even more irritated if they watch a Flash movie and *never* see their information scent validated at all, or if the movie distracts them from reaching their query goals (**Figure 5.4**).

NOTE A *splash page* is a web page that typically consists of either a Flash animation and a redirect to a new page after the animation finishes, or a link to skip the Flash animation (Skip Intro).

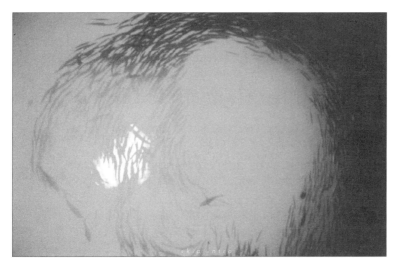

Figure 5.4 This screenshot is the beginning of a Flash movie on a website's home page, with the call to action, *skip intro*, barely visible at the bottom of the screen. What type of products or services do you believe this site offers?

Videos often decrease search usability by delaying, diminishing, distracting from, or hiding the scent of information.

Even the most experienced web users become easily irritated with Flash videos, as the "The Cost of Assuming User Expectations" case study illustrates.

CASE STUDY
THE COST OF ASSUMING USER EXPECTATIONS

A software client wanted to increase the search usability of his website, and he wanted to determine why the site was not converting well. Since this client's minimum purchase price was over $100,000, he was not targeting small or medium-sized companies. The specific primary persona was the head of an information technology (IT) department who made purchasing decisions. Therefore, we only recruited people who fit this description as participants in the usability test. All participants had considerable web experience.

People who commonly visited our client's site had the following goals:

- Find a vendor source for products or technology licensing (transactional and informational)
- Quickly get a datasheet on desired technology and/or product (navigational)
- Purchase or license products/technology (transactional)

Nowhere in these goals is the word *video* or *Flash* mentioned. Nevertheless, the client used many Flash movies on the site, especially on the home page. Right away, we knew we were going to tell our client to sink the splash page, or at least decrease the amount of screen real estate allocated to the large Flash video. Our client insisted that their target audience absolutely loved the Flash video. IT people love to watch cool movies, they claimed. Plus management insisted that the use of advanced technology on a site gave their brand more credibility.

Our usability test began on the client's home page. Here were some of the responses to the Flash video:

- "I don't have time for this. Quit wasting my [expletive] time...." (Participant abandoned the task.)
- "The site wastes space. I am very busy... I want to get down to business. I want to see things. These light waves—this is just distracting." (Participant abandoned the task.)
- "This graphic takes up way too much space and doesn't give me any information. It doesn't tell me anything and keeps up this annoying flashing when I'm trying to do something else." (Participant abandoned the task.)
- "What the [expletive] is this?" (Participant abandoned the task.)
- "Are you [expletive] kidding me? I don't have time for this...." (Participant abandoned the task.)

Unfortunately, our client did not accept our findings, even after we played audio recordings of the sessions. Six months later, when we viewed our client's updated website, almost all of the Flash had been removed. Even the large Flash video on the home page was smaller, and more room was made for keyword-focused copy.

Moral of the story? Advanced Internet users do not automatically wish to see the latest and greatest technology on a website merely because they are advanced Internet users. Don't assume. Test.

■ SEARCH LISTINGS AND TRANSACTIONAL QUERIES

In terms of individual parts of a transactional search listing, transactional listings are similar to informational search listings. The URL is less important to searchers because the information and the associated activity is the main target, not necessarily the URL. Keyword research, A/B testing, and multivariate testing can show you if interactivity keywords should appear in the listing, as shown in **Figure 5.5**:

FIGURE 5.5 For a transactional query, the two most important items in a search listing are the (1) title-tag content, and (2) the page snippet or meta-tag description. Notice that the activity words *play, set,* and *try* appear in the listing description, encouraging searchers to click the link to the website.

NOTE *A/B split testing* is a method where a baseline control item is compared to a number of single-variable items in order to determine the best option. For example, you can compare different font sizes in a headline to determine which size users respond to most. *Multivariate testing* (also known as *multivariable testing*), as the name implies, compares multiple variables. For example, a multivariate test can reveal the best font size, font color, and number of words in a web page headline.

■ TRANSACTIONAL QUERY INDICATORS

Your Web analytics data and keyword research data can help you determine which query words show transactional intent. Some transactional query indicators include:

- Specific interaction verbs (*buy, find, search, download, play, view, log in, register, enroll, subscribe, join, apply, contact, chat,* and so on).

- Nouns that are associated with some type of activity (*games, movies, music, recipes, slide shows, demo, tour, quote, calculator, software* or the software name, and so on).

- File extensions for nontext files (.jpg for photos, .mp3 for music, and .mpg for videos) and file compression (.zip for Windows computers and .sit for Macintosh computers).

■ OPTIMIZING FOR TRANSACTIONAL QUERIES

Here are some general guidelines for optimizing your website to accommodate transactional queries:

- The primary call to action should be painfully obvious to both site owners and searchers. For example, if you want searchers to download a file, the word *download* should be part of the hyperlink, and that hyperlink should look clickable (**Figures 5.6** and **5.7**). The transactional scent of information should be maintained from a search results page to the landing page. Chapter 8, "Search Usability Is Everyone's Job," discusses calls to action in greater detail.

Apple - **Safari - Download**
Download Safari 3 and experience the world's fastest, easiest-to-use web browser . Free for Mac and PC.
www.apple.com/**safari/download/** - 12k - Cached - Similar pages

Title   *URL*   *Description*

Figure 5.6 In the search listing, the call to action is seen in the title tag, the description (which is the page's meta-tag content in this instance), and the URL.

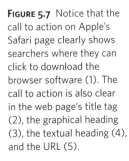

Figure 5.7 Notice that the call to action on Apple's Safari page clearly shows searchers where they can click to download the browser software (1). The call to action is also clear in the web page's title tag (2), the graphical heading (3), the textual heading (4), and the URL (5).

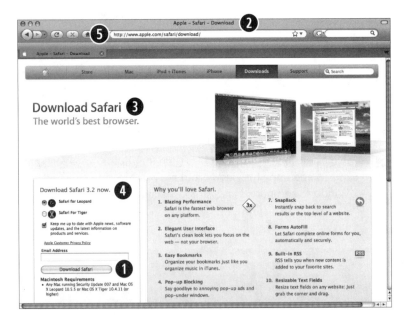

- Include desired activity words in the title tag on key pages. For example, if you offer a specific search page on your site, then make sure you use the word *search* or *find* in the title, heading, URL, and description of the page. Likewise, if you have a login page on your site, such as an email login, make sure you use the word *login* in the title, heading, URL, and description of your page.

- Don't assume searchers want to take an action without initiating it themselves. In other words, don't start playing a video or sound file unless the searcher specifically indicates that he/she wishes to watch the video or listen to the sound file.

- Focus groups are not always the best source of information for feedback on interactivity and multimedia because the focus group leader, not the user, guides the interactivity. Furthermore, a focus group typically shows initial reactions to an interactive feature, not long-term effects.

CASE STUDY
OFFICIAL FAN SITE

One of the most revealing field studies we performed was for an official Frank Sinatra fan site. The site had many sound clips that people could listen to at their leisure...except for one file on the site's home page that automatically played every time the home page loaded.

The site owners thought the sound file was really cool. When fans first visited the site, they also thought the sound file was cool. You could see that they liked it from the expressions on their faces.

Over time, though, as we worked on iterative designs and functionality, we watched test participants become irritated with the home page. At some point, most participants asked if they could unplug the speakers or turn off the volume before the test commenced.

We quickly learned that sound files might impress new visitors but alienate repeat visitors. Had we not observed one-on-one user activity on this site over time, we never would have learned this about the site's target audience. The site still uses sound files, but a sound clip does not play unless a site visitor specifically requests to hear it.

■ CONCLUSION

Key points in this chapter:

- Transactional queries are those in which searchers wish to perform some sort of online or offline activity beyond merely reading.

- Transactional queries are very important to site owners because they capture searchers at a critical point in the buying process: when they are ready to buy.

- Certain verbs such as *download, search, find, log in, chat, apply, buy*, and so forth indicate transactional intent.

- Transactional keyword phrases do not always contain a verb. Certain nouns such as *video(s), picture(s)* or *pic(s), music*, and *game(s)* also show transactional intent because they imply watching, hearing, and playing, respectively.

- Likewise, file extensions such as .jpg for photos, .mp3 for music, and .mpg for videos are a strong indicator of transactional intent.

- On key pages within a site, place the word that describes searchers' desired activity in the title tag content. For example, an advanced search page should contain the words *search* or *find* in the title tag content. Pages where searchers can download software should contain the word *download* in the title tag.

- When searchers demonstrate transactional intent, the corresponding landing page (after clicking a search listing) should contain their desired call to action above the fold. This call to action should stand out on the page. In other words, searchers should not have to work very hard to complete their desired activity.

- Don't delay, diminish, distract from, or hide the scent of information by initiating an action (such as playing a video). Let users initiate their desired activities.

CHAPTER 6

THE SCENT OF INFORMATION AND LANDING PAGES

After searchers click a link to your website from a search engine, they have two choices: They can either stay on your site, or they can abandon it. One reason searchers stay on a website is the scent of information. If they see their user-generated scent of information (keywords) on a website's landing page, they believe the page will help them reach their goals: where they want to go, what they want to learn, and what they want to do. Searchers become confident that the landing page is giving them what they need. The result is a great user experience, more sales and conversions, and a positive brand impact.

Searching does not end after a person clicks a link from a search engine results page (SERP) to a website. People still look for desired content once they enter and browse a website, and they exhibit some specific behaviors while they are looking. By considering these behaviors and applying some simple techniques, you can build your website to help users follow the scent of information.

■ SCANNING BEHAVIOR

The vast majority of users do not read web pages word by word. Instead, they scan pages for individual keywords and keyword phrases. If users arrive on your site and do not see their desired content after a quick scan, they will abandon the site and move on to another. Recent studies show that users only read about 20 percent of the words on a web page. Therefore, if users arrive on your site via the commercial web search engines, important keywords and calls to action need to be featured prominently (above the fold) on web pages.

NOTE See Jakob Nielsen's "How Little Do Users Read?" at http://www.useit.com/alertbox/percent-text-read.html. The article contains a link to the full academic paper.

It is not enough to call attention to keywords on your web pages. For your site to be successful, users must perform certain actions on it. Calls to action should stand out on the page as well. What do you want users to do after they find their desired content? Add to cart? Enroll or register? Log in? Subscribe to your blog? Fill out a form?

A *call to action* is something you wish users to do when they land on a page. Most web pages contain multiple calls to action. As an example, let's use a product page from an e-commerce website.

The primary call to action on a product page is *Add to cart*. A *primary call to action* is the one action you most wish users to do. If users are not ready to respond to your primary call to action, what do you want them to do instead? Abandon your website? Of course not. You want them to stay on your site and maybe purchase a similar item. So the secondary call to action might be to click links to alternative products. What if users do not wish to answer the secondary call to action? What do you want them to do? Call a customer service agent?

Identifying and prioritizing calls to action for every page on your site might seem like an exhausting exercise. However, site visitors will not *Add to cart* unless you make it easy for them. And they will not look at additional items unless you provide links to those related items. Site visitors need to see both keywords and the main calls to action with a quick scan.

How can you call attention to both keywords and calls to action on a web page? First, you should identify and prioritize the primary, secondary, and third-level calls to action on each type of web page. **Table 6.1** shows a simple spreadsheet layout for this process:

TABLE 6.1 Identifying and prioritizing calls to action on web pages

PAGE NAME	CALL TO ACTION 1	CALL TO ACTION 2	CALL TO ACTION 3
Product A	Add to cart	Watch product video	Click links to related items
Product B	Add to cart	View larger image	Click links to related items
Contact Us	Fill out contact form	Email customer service	Call toll-free number

Second, as you design each element on a page, format the primary call to action so that it stands out. The following list includes some ways to draw attention to an item on a web page (ordered from the least attention grabbing to most attention grabbing):

- Dimmed text
- Italics
- Bold
- Larger font/typeface (typically in page headings)
- Border
- Color (warm colors advance and cool colors recede; eyes naturally move to heavy color saturation and a large number of colors, and so on)
- Graphic images (curves versus straight lines; photos of faces or people; effects that indicate a dimension change such as beveling, embossing, shadows, and so on)
- Sound
- Animation/movement

The secondary call to action should be subtler than the primary one, but the secondary call to action should still be featured prominently on a page. The third-level call to action should be even more subtle than the secondary one, and so on. **Figure 6.1** shows the formatting of the various calls to action on a product page.

FIGURE 6.1 An e-commerce site's product page.

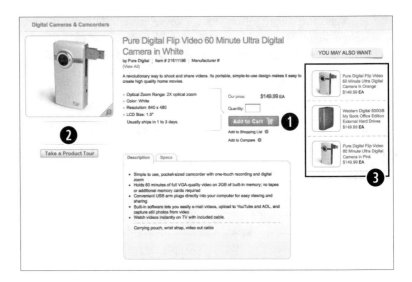

The primary call to action is *Add to cart*. It is formatted as a graphic image in a warm color. The image has rounded corners, which makes it stand out on a website that has a grid layout, and it has an icon. It is larger than other navigation buttons. The shading and slight bevel add unique dimension. And it is placed near the center of the screen surrounded by some extra white space.

The secondary call to action is either to enlarge the product photo or to take the product tour. These calls to action are easy to spot because online shoppers always want to see a photo or a video of the product they are purchasing. Therefore, users have come to expect a link for such views. Additionally, photos typically contain millions of colors. The product photo is the largest photo on the page. The curved magnifying glass (icon) link to view the larger photo is located within the photo's border. Note that the magnifying glass conforms to prior experiences among users. Therefore, the site visitor need not spend effort to "decode" the icon. User icons match users' expectations and prior experiences. Users do not have to click that icon to view a larger photo. They can click the product photo as well. Both the magnifying glass link and the product tour button use a dimmed color, which helps the primary call to action stand out.

The third-level call to action is to view related items. This call to action is formatted as text links and associated thumbnail photos, which are located in the right column of the page. Note that placement on the right side conforms to site visitors' expected pattern of page reading: left to right. Thus, a third-level call to action fits best to the right of a secondary call to action. In a text-like document, task follows our left-right, top-down reading habit (in Romance languages). Note that Arabic and Hebrew are read right-left, then top-down. Follow the expectations of whatever language you serve.

Once you have formatted some page prototypes, you can conduct a variety of usability tests to determine their effectiveness. Eye-tracking studies can tell you whether users' eyes are focusing on keywords and calls to action. Performance tests can tell you which formats yield the most clicks and the most conversions. Even free exploration tests can let you know if calls to action are annoying, too subtle, or just right. Let's look in greater detail at a couple of usability tests you can conduct to determine the mental models of web searchers.

Anticipate Searcher Needs with Usability Tests

One way to determine searchers' mental models of your web pages is to perform an expectancy test. An expectancy test will also reveal searchers' expectations about your web page's content.

To perform this test, you first will need to gather examples of listings from the commercial web search engines, using your most important keyword phrases shown in **Figure 6.2**.

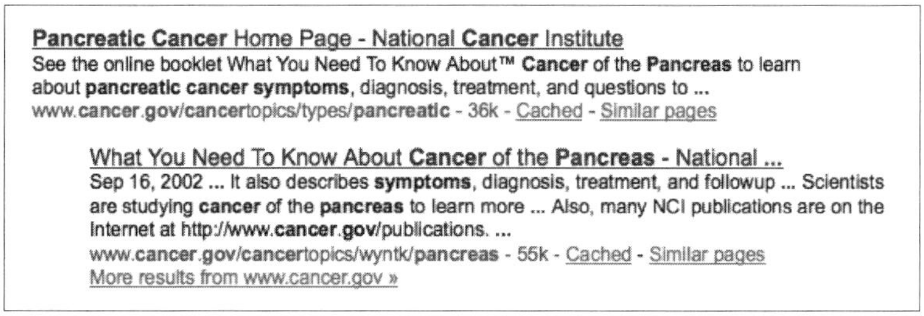

> **Note** A *performance test* evaluates the effectiveness of site navigation, labeling and terminology, organization of content, task flow, error handling, and calls to action on a website. Performance tests can tell you how many users complete the assigned task, how many steps they took to complete the task, time spent, and potential roadblocks. You will learn how to do a *free exploration test* in Chapter 9, "How To Improve Your Website's Search Usability."

Pancreatic Cancer Home Page - National **Cancer** Institute
See the online booklet What You Need To Know About™ **Cancer** of the **Pancreas** to learn about **pancreatic cancer symptoms**, diagnosis, treatment, and questions to ...
www.**cancer.gov**/cancertopics/types/**pancreatic** - 36k - Cached - Similar pages

What You Need To Know About **Cancer** of the **Pancreas** - National ...
Sep 16, 2002 ... It also describes **symptoms**, diagnosis, treatment, and followup ... Scientists are studying **cancer** of the **pancreas** to learn more ... Also, many NCI publications are on the Internet at http://www.**cancer.gov**/publications. ...
www.**cancer.gov**/cancertopics/wyntk/**pancreas** - 55k - Cached - Similar pages
More results from www.cancer.gov »

Figure 6.2 Google listings for the keyword phrase *pancreatic cancer symptoms.* These listings appear specifically for the National Cancer Institute's website.

If you are having a difficult time finding your site's listings in Google's search results, you can easily find them by performing an advanced search. Type in your targeted keyword phrase followed by *site:* and your domain name (no space between the colon and your domain name). For example, the listings in Figure 6.2 were located using the following query:

pancreatic cancer symptoms site:www.cancer.gov

How to perform the expectancy usability test:

1. Present participants with one or two search engine listings, such as the ones shown in Figure 6.2.

2. Ask participants, "What content do you expect to see if you click this link?" Have them explain why they expect to see specific content.

> **Note** If you want to find the search listing for an exact keyword phrase on your site, enclose the keyword phrase in quotation marks. For example, if you want to find the exact phrase *pancreatic cancer symptoms* on the National Cancer Institute site, the Google query will be *"pancreatic cancer symptoms" site:www.cancer.gov.*

3. Ask participants, "What do you think will happen if you click this link?" Have them explain why they believe something will or will not happen.

4. Perform this test for navigational, informational, and transactional keyword phrases.

NOTE Different ways of using the five-second usability test will be discussed in Chapter 9, "Search Usability and Your Site's Success." You can find out more about Jared's five-second test at www.uie.com/articles/five_second_test/

Normally, in an expectancy test, you do not tell participants whether their answer is right or wrong because you are simply determining their mental models. However, we also want to know how well or poorly the landing page meets searcher expectations. So follow up the expectancy test with Jared Spool's five-second usability test, a test which is used to gather initial impressions and to quickly measure how a content page performs with users.

How to perform Jared Spool's five-second usability test:

1. Show the user the landing page that corresponds directly to the search listing.

2. Count five seconds.

3. Close the window or take the landing page away from the user.

4. Ask the user:
   - Was this content what you expected to see after you clicked the search listing? Why or why not?
   - What (content) did you expect to see but did not see?
   - What (content) did you want to see? Why did you want to see it?

What you are trying to determine is whether users easily spotted their scent of information (keywords). Were users able to see their information scent validated on the landing page? If they did not, why didn't they see it? Where on the landing page did they expect to see keywords and associated images?

If the scent of information is too weak or disappears, people will abandon your website.

Sometimes, after the initial five-second test, you might allow test participants to view the landing page for an additional 8–10 seconds to gather more details. But still carefully note what they did and did not notice within the first five seconds of viewing the page.

If a web page was optimized well for search engine visibility, keyword usage on the landing page will be obvious. You will commonly see keywords in the title tags, visible body text (headings, paragraphs, breadcrumb links, and so on), and the URL. However, you might not always see keywords on the page because the design team might have unwittingly blocked the information scent.

Remember, if the scent of information is too weak or disappears, people will abandon your website. Let's look at some ways that web designers, and search engine marketers, might unwittingly delay, diminish, or block the scent of information.

Avoid the Iceberg Effect

On many websites, the most important content tends to get buried far below the fold, like the proverbial iceberg, with only 10 percent of page content visible at the top of the screen (**Figure 6.3**).

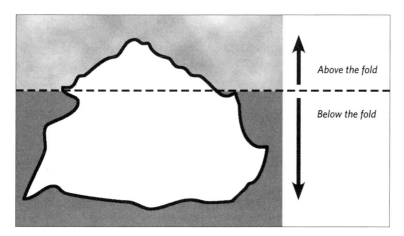

Above the fold

Below the fold

FIGURE 6.3 The iceberg effect

When web searchers land on an *iceberg* page, it does not appear to have their desired content. The scent of information is missing and they abandon the site. So if you find that important pages have a high *bounce rate*, see if the page layout might be hiding keywords.

Some web designers and developers inadvertently hide the scent of information when they use a file tab layout as shown in **Figure 6.4** on the next page. The default file tab displays product details. If a user clicks another file tab, the product details content will disappear and different text will appear in its place. Although this particular design strategy is useful for preserving screen real estate, it can hide the scent of information—keywords.

NOTE *Bounce rate* is a term used in website analytics that refers to the effectiveness of an entry page. More specifically, it is a percentage of pages that are viewed once—when a site visitor lands on an entry page and then abandons the site after only viewing that entry page. It is typically calculated as:

$$\frac{\text{Number of single page accesses}}{\text{Total number of entries}} \times 100 = \text{Bounce rate}$$

FIGURE 6.4 File tabs and their corresponding layers. Product review content is not visible to web searcher (1) until they click the "Reviews" link (2). If the website owner wants searchers to read product reviews, the scent of information (the "Reviews" link) should be located at the tip of the iceberg.

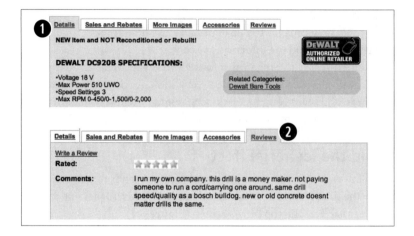

An even worse situation can occur if the file tabs appear below the fold. In this situation, not only are important keywords invisible to users, but the links that lead to their desired information disappear. To preserve the scent of information on pages that use this layout, make sure the most important keywords are available above the fold in the short product description. If you cannot place searchers' most important keywords above the fold, then make sure the file tabs appear above the fold (**Figure 6.5**). The file tab links let your target audience know that their desired content might be available on that web page.

FIGURE 6.5 Keep file tabs visible above the fold to provide an information scent.

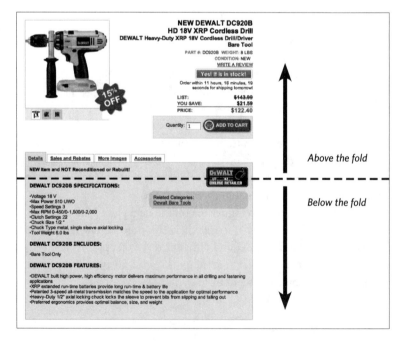

Another effective way to maintain the scent of information on a long web page is to write multiple HTML headlines using keywords. At the top of the web page, make sure there are hypertext links to those headings. This format is highly useful for screen readers as well (**Figure 6.6**).

NOTE A *screen reader* is software that interprets and reads (aloud) content that is displayed on a computer screen. Computer users who are blind or visually impaired typically use screen readers to navigate websites and read site content. Visually impaired users can call up a list of on-the-page headings and jump directly to the section of the page that contains their desired content.

FIGURE 6.6 Provide links above the fold to the content below the fold.

To maintain the scent of information, make sure that the words on file tabs and hypertext links are reinforced in the text the users see after they click them. If the words are not reinforced, users feel the links are misleading.

Avoid Misleading Links

Users become frustrated if they follow a scent of information and it leads them down the wrong path. If users believe that a website is deceitful, they will view that brand as being untrustworthy.

Suppose you are driving to Phoenix, Arizona, to meet potential customers. You are looking forward to meeting these prospects because they have actively sought out your products and services. As you are driving, you see the sign shown in **Figure 6.7**.

FIGURE 6.7 Road sign pointing to Phoenix, Arizona.

The scent of information in this sign is straightforward. If you wish to go to Tucson, then you drive straight ahead. If you wish to go to Phoenix, then you must make a right turn. The sign provides two visual cues as the scent of information: city names (text) and arrows (images) indicating the direction you must drive to reach your destination.

Now suppose your competitor wants you to miss your meeting with your prospect. He replaces the sign shown in Figure 6.7 with the sign in **Figure 6.8**.

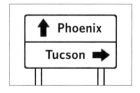

FIGURE 6.8 Sign showing the wrong directions

The directions are reversed. Drivers who follow this misleading scent of information will drive toward the wrong city—wasting time and gas money, maybe even losing new customers. Even if a person notices that the sign's directions are reversed, he is distracted from reaching his destination because of his confusion. And this is how users feel when they use a website with misleading or mislabeled links—confused, distracted, annoyed, and frustrated.

Many Flash sites appear to be misleading links in search listings because searchers do not see keywords in the search listing also appearing on the landing page (**Figure 6.9**). What product, service, or information does this home page offer? Help desk software? Accounting software? Press release services? Babysitting services? Or maybe skip intro services? In this instance, the Flash technology is not the problem since Google has been able to crawl Flash sites for many years. The problem is how Flash technology is being used—web developers and site owners do not always consider searchers' scanning behavior when they build these sites.

FIGURE 6.9 This web page formatted in Flash does not contain any keywords.

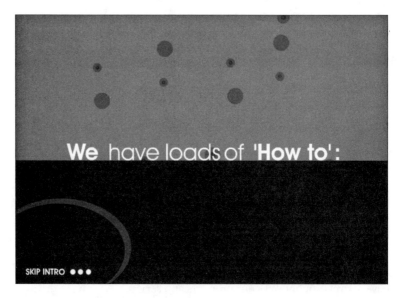

On a website, a misleading scent of information can be a costly mistake. Not only will it confuse current site visitors, it will also alienate new visitors. Even if you did not intend to mislead site visitors, they still might perceive your site as deceptive. People will not give you their personal information and credit card numbers if they feel your website is untrustworthy.

■ FOSTER ORIENTING BEHAVIOR

Orienting is a behavior in which people use cues to determine where they are located. In the physical world, people might determine their location by using a map, road signs (**Figure 6.10**), symbols, words, a global positioning system (GPS), or a combination.

FIGURE 6.10 The stop sign, the painted line on the road, and the word *stop* painted on the road are all visual cues that help drivers orient themselves at this intersection.

Orienting is something people do without realizing it. For example, when you ride in an elevator, the lights above the doors communicate which floor you are on. If you see the number *"3"* light up, you know the elevator is on the third floor. If you see the letter "L" light up, you know the elevator is on the lobby level. The elevator lights are *you are here* cues that help you orient yourself within a building.

The presence of easily scanned you are here *cues makes users feel your site is trustworthy and credible.*

Likewise, there are many *you are here* cues that can help users determine their location within a website. After people click a link from a search engine results page, they scan the web page for *you are here* cues. Ideally, people should be able to orient themselves on a web page with little or no effort. And they should be able to orient themselves within five to 10 seconds after a page loads.

The presence of easily scanned *you are here* cues helps instill trust and credibility in your site. As users click, the site should communicate to them that they are getting closer to their goal. *You are here* cues can provide that feedback, especially if they are based on query words. In addition, consistently implementing *you are here* cues helps users accomplish their tasks more quickly and efficiently.

To determine how easily searchers orient themselves on a web page, use the five-second usability test again:

1. Show the user the landing page that corresponds directly to the search listing.

2. Count five seconds.

3. Close the window or take the landing page away from the user.

4. Ask the user:
   - Whose website are you viewing? How did you determine this?
   - What section, if any, of the site are you viewing? How did you determine this?
   - What content is available on this page? How did you determine this?
   - How confident are you that your desired content is on this page?

5. Ask the following questions if participants indicated that they did *not* see their desired content:
   - Do you believe that this page will lead you to your desired content?
   - How did you determine this?
   - How confident are you that this page will lead you to your desired content?

Figure 6.11 shows the places that people typically look at to orient themselves within a website.

1. **Title tag.** In Firefox and Internet Explorer, a web page's title-tag content is visible at the top of the screen and in the file tab underneath the address bar in the latest web browsers.

2. **URL.** In an ideal situation, the URL should reflect page content, especially for navigational queries.

3. **Logo and tagline.** People expect to be told whose site they are visiting in the upper left corner of a web page.

FIGURE 6.11 Areas on a web page where site visitors scan to establish a sense of place.

4. **Locational breadcrumb links.** These links communicate to users where they are within a website's hierarchy and what page they are currently viewing.

5. **Page heading.** Site visitors use the page heading to orient themselves largely due to wording, font size, font color, surrounding white space, and location on the screen.

6. **Main content at the top of the page.** People scan text at the top of the page for their targeted keywords. If they used a transactional word for images (such as *photos*) or *videos*, they expect to see non-text representations of those transactional words as well.

7. **Navigation buttons.** Current page and/or section of the site is highlighted.

You are here cues are very important to web searchers because when they click a link from a search engine results page, they do not always enter the site via the home page. In all likelihood, they arrive on a page somewhere in the middle a site. If the search engine correctly interprets searchers' intent, then searchers should land on a page that contains their desired content, or leads them to their desired content. Let's look at an example.

Figure 6.12 shows the top Google search results for the informational query *breast cancer tests*. Notice that both listings from the National Cancer Institute site do not lead to the home page.

FIGURE 6.12 If web searchers click a link from a search engine results page, they often land on a page in the middle of a website.

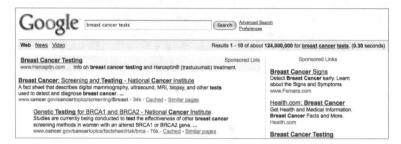

The first search listing in Figure 6.12 leads to a category page. Google has interpreted the plural form of the word *test* to mean that searchers might be looking for a list of breast cancer tests (**Figure 6.13**), which the following landing page provides.

FIGURE 6.13 Landing page after a searcher clicks the link in the first search listing in Figure 6.12. The searcher is landing on a category page in the middle of a site, not the home page.

Now let's review the questions asked during a five-second usability test to see if and how users were able to determine their location within the National Cancer Institute's website.

- **Whose website are you viewing? How did you determine this?**

  Participants said they were viewing the National Cancer Institute's website. They specifically mentioned the logo and text in the masthead area as key indicators that they were viewing a web page on the National Cancer Institute site.

- **What section, if any, of the site are you viewing? How did you determine this?**

    Participants believed they were in the Cancer Topics area of the site because they saw the navigation button labeled Cancer Topics highlighted. They also believed they were in a breast cancer area of the site because of the large page heading.

- **What content is available on this page? How did you determine this?**

    Participants believed they were viewing a page about breast cancer tests, the very keywords that they typed into Google. The large page heading, the logo, and the organization name all led them to believe that their desired content was available on this page.

- **How confident are you that your desired content is on this page?**

    All participants were confident that their desired content was on the page, or at least on the site. This particular landing page contains easy-to-find links to guide people to more detailed information on other pages within the site. The presence and formatting of the secondary heading *Mammography* helped increase user confidence (**Figure 6.14**).

Mammography

Screening Mammograms: Questions and Answers
A fact sheet that defines screening mammograms and their benefits and limitations. Discusses mammogram screening guidelines and risk factors for breast cancer. National Cancer Institute Fact Sheet 5.28

FIGURE 6.14 When test participants were shown the National Cancer Institute's category page about breast cancer tests for five seconds, almost all participants were able to establish where they were within the NCI website.

Websites that facilitate scanning and orienting help searchers reach their goals more quickly and efficiently; increase user confidence, trust, and credibility; and can help sites achieve and maintain top search engine positions. However, not all behaviors that people exhibit when they look for content indicates a positive user experience. Some search behaviors indicate a negative user experience due to a lost scent of information.

■ POGO-STICKING: NEGATIVE SEARCH BEHAVIOR

NOTE For details on pogo-sticking, see "Galleries: The Hardest Working Web Pages on Your Site" by Jared Spool at http://www.uie.com/articles/galleries/. Spool found that the more users exhibited pogo-sticking behavior on a website, the less they purchased.

Pogo-sticking is a browsing behavior where users jump up and down the hierarchy of a website to find their desired content. If users exhibit considerable pogo-sticking behavior, they are less likely to purchase, download, or answer any primary call to action on your website. Here is an example of pogo-sticking behavior.

Suppose a searcher wants to purchase a digital camera. He is viewing a category page labeled "Digital Cameras." This category page contains a list of thumbnail photos and corresponding text links to individual product pages. One camera looks promising. So he clicks the link to view details about the camera. He doesn't see exactly what he wants and clicks back to the category page. He sees another camera that he likes. So he clicks the link to a different product page. The camera is too expensive, so he clicks back to the category page. And so on. This searcher is exhibiting pogo-sticking behavior, jumping back and forth between a category page and individual product pages as **Figure 6.15** illustrates.

FIGURE 6.15 A searcher clicks back and forth between a product page and category pages, pogo-sticking to find the information they want.

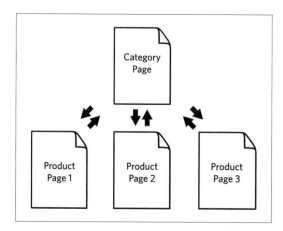

Usability testing is crucial to determining whether users are pogo-sticking, because web analytics data can be misleading. Many analytics packages are designed to calculate the average number of page views per visitor, but the packages are not set up to determine if the increased page views are due to pogo-sticking behavior.

Clickstream analysis might help you identify pages where pogo-sticking occurs. To help users succeed in getting their desired content, site owners should understand *where* people are pogo-sticking on a site, and *why* people are pogo-sticking. Usability testing will give you those answers.

NOTE A *clickstream* is a recording of what a site visitor clicks while browsing a website.

Usability testing is crucial to determining whether users are pogo-sticking, because web analytics data can be misleading.

Remember, management might be happy to see increased page views. But if site visitors are pogo-sticking, they are having a negative user experience. Most users buy products without pogo-sticking at all.

■ CONCLUSION

Key points in this chapter:

- Users only read about 20 percent of the words on a web page. Users don't read; they scan web pages for their targeted keywords. So don't make users work too hard to find desired content.

- Conduct expectancy tests to determine web searchers' mental model of your landing page after they view various search listings.

- Web searchers want see their query words and calls to action featured prominently on web pages.

- Identifying and prioritizing calls to action for every web page on your site is important for converting site visitors into buyers.

- Make the primary call to action the most noticeable call to action on a page. The placement and formatting of secondary and third-level calls to action should be more subtle.

- Web designers and search engine marketers might delay, diminish, or block the scent of information by hiding desired content below the fold and in invisible layers.

- Many Flash sites appear to be misleading links in search listings because searchers do not see keywords in the search listing also being used on the landing page.

- *Orienting* is a behavior in which people use cues to determine where they are located with little or no effort.

- Site visitors should be able to orient themselves within five to 10 seconds after a page loads.

- *Pogo-sticking* is a browsing behavior in which users jump up and down the hierarchy of a website to find their desired information. This behavior can be an indication of a lost information scent.

CHAPTER 7

SEARCH USABILITY AND YOUR SITE'S SUCCESS

This chapter illustrates how improving search usability can benefit websites that sell products and services as well as those that sell advertising on their web pages. We'll also look at how you can use search usability to support customers of existing products and services and how you can improve the bottom line when you reduce employees' time on the company intranet by improving the findability of content.

Additionally, we examine common measures of success and web analytics that might look easy to interpret, but can be deceiving if you don't understand the thinking behind users' actions.

■ SEARCH USABILITY METRICS BY SITE TYPE

From a business perspective, a website can have a variety of specific primary goals, such as increasing conversions. For example, the primary goal of an e-commerce site is to increase online purchasing. Similar is true for nonprofit websites (increase memberships) and business-to-business websites (generate more leads). The primary business goal for news and information websites is to increase page views so they can charge more for advertising.

The following sections outline business models that involve making financial and traffic assumptions. The take-away from the models is the thinking behind the numbers, not the numbers themselves. Adjust the models to calculate ROI that more accurately reflects your website's potential. A model is a representation of a process designed to aid in understanding and/or predicting results. The following formulas are an example of one type of business model to predict daily profit of an e-commerce website.

$$(5{,}000 \text{ visitors/day} \times 2\% \text{ conversion}) \times \$20 \text{ sale} = \$2{,}000 \text{ gross sales}$$

$$\text{Gross sales} \times 20\% \text{ profit} = \$400 \text{ profit}$$

When developing your assumptions for your models, keep in mind that the more accurate your values, the more accurate your annual revenue prediction will be. Your predicted annual revenue will dramatically compound any poorly chosen monthly values used in your model. For example, if your monthly revenue is off by $10K, your annual revenue will be off by $120K. Keep this in mind as you serve up the predicted annual revenue to management or to your client.

Selling Products and Services with Search Usability

Let's take a look at how we leverage search usability (SEO and web usability) to contribute to the bottom line for websites with a primary goal of selling products or services.

Selling products and services includes both commercial tangibles like sneakers and intangibles like cell phone services. Nonprofits have just as much to gain as commercial sites from the "products and services" model if you consider your items, such as annual memberships, an intangible item. Let's first take a look at factors that will determine the ROI of your search usability investment for selling products, services, and memberships.

For example, to calculate the monthly revenue in the products and service model, you use the following formula:

$$\text{(Monthly unique visits} \times \text{Page view to conversion ratio)} \times$$
$$\text{Average purchase} = \text{Monthly revenue}$$

- **Page view to conversion ratio:** The page view to conversion ratio states that of X number of unique visitors who land on a page that allows for a transaction (such as an add to cart page) you can expect Y to make a transaction. If you were to apply this to a website that sells ear muffs, it would look something like this: of 100 unique visitors who land on the ear muffs page, you can assume one visitor will buy the ear muffs. The assumed page view to conversion ratio in this case is 100 to 1, or 1 percent.

- **Current and prospective traffic:** This is the traffic you currently have and incremental gains to project future traffic. In this example, we will use 100,000 as the baseline for the monthly unique visits and incremental gains of 5 percent to estimate prospective traffic generated by SEO efforts.

- **Monthly unique visits:** You use this number to establish a baseline for monthly unique visits. You can establish this number by looking at your web analytics. When establishing your baseline, be sure to take into account seasonality and other factors that might skew your data. You should establish a number that will help predict accurate marketing results. Data that is atypical and not representative of your monthly activity will result in an error-prone predictive model.

  Historical data from your website is the best option for building your models. If don't have historical data to work with, try to establish a baseline using third-party research data or, if available, data from a comparable sister site. Worse case scenario, you might have to SWAG your monthly unique visits before you can generate your own historical data.

- **Average purchase:** If your website only features one product, priced at $50, then your value of average purchase will be easy to figure out. If you have other variables, take a look at what your web analytics are telling you, talk to marketing to establish a value of an average purchase you can use to predict results.

- **Monthly revenue:** Monthly revenue is the result of multiplying predefined quantities:

$$\text{(Monthly unique visits} \times \text{Page view to conversion ratio)} \times$$
$$\text{Average purchase} = \text{Monthly revenue}$$

> **NOTE** SWAG is an acronym for *Stupid Wild Ass Guess, Smart Wild Ass Guess,* and/or *Scientific Wild Ass Guess.* Ideally, your SWAG will be closer to the scientific end of the spectrum. If you find yourself in a SWAG situation, try using a range of numbers that shows a conservative view and an aggressive view.

When you plug in the values of 100,000 monthly unique visits, a 1 percent page view to conversion ratio, and a $50 average purchase, the monthly revenue looks like this:

$$(100,000 \times 1\%) \times 50 = \$50,000$$

- **Annual revenue:** You calculate annual revenue by multiplying your monthly revenue by 12.

Now that we have covered the factors, let's take a look at **Table 7.1** to see what we can expect in terms of annual revenue from an e-commerce website by increasing traffic using SEO.

The model in **Tables 7.1**, **7.2**, and **7.3** uses the example of an e-commerce site that sells a tangible item at an average purchase of $50. "Average purchase" can easily be replaced with "average cost of service" for an e-commerce site that sells intangibles or "average cost of membership" for a nonprofit site whose organization is supported by member contributions. "Average purchase" can also be substituted with "average value of lead" for websites with the primary goal of delivering leads to a sales force. You can modify the headings in these tables according to your business model.

TABLE 7.1 Products and services model with SEO improvement

CURRENT AND PROSPECTIVE TRAFFIC	MONTHLY UNIQUE VISITS	PAGE VIEW TO CONVERSION RATIO	AVERAGE PURCHASE	MONTHLY REVENUE	ANNUAL REVENUE
Current traffic	100,000	1.00%	$50	$50,000	$600,000
Plus 5%	105,000	1.00%	$50	$52,500	$630,000
Plus 10%	110,000	1.00%	$50	$55,000	$660,000
Plus 15%	115,000	1.00%	$50	$57,500	$690,000

NOTE A 5 percent increase in SEO traffic resulting in an increase of 5,000 monthly unique visits may not be realistic for smaller e-commerce websites. This doesn't mean that your site won't benefit from SEO efforts, it just means that it might take longer to achieve your ROI.

The only factor that changes in Table 7.1 is the monthly unique visits. Even at a 1 percent conversion rate and an average purchase of $50, you see the increase of $90,000 ($690,00 – $600,000) in annual revenue with a 15 percent increase in SEO traffic.

Using the same model, let's take a look at annual results when you improve the search usability of your website by making it easier for users to find desired products and complete tasks such as *add to cart*.

In **Table 7.2**, the factor that changes is the page view to conversion ratio. At an incremental gain of .25 percent, retaining the average purchase of $50 and the 100,000 monthly unique visits results in an increase of $450,000 ($1,050,000 – $600,000) in annual revenue when comparing an increase of 1.00 percent to 1.75 percent page view to conversion ratio.

Table 7.2 assumes that there is no increase in the monthly unique visits from SEO efforts, but rather the increase in annual revenue hinges solely on the page view to conversion ratio that was boosted by improving the search usability of the page. The boost in page view to conversion ratio might be a result of making the "add to cart" button more apparent by

- Removing distracting elements from the page
- Increasing the size of the "add to cart" button
- Using a more eye-catching color for the "add to cart" button

TABLE 7.2 Products and services model with increased usability

CURRENT AND PROSPECTIVE TRAFFIC	MONTHLY UNIQUE VISITS	PAGE VIEW TO CONVERSION RATIO	AVERAGE PURCHASE	MONTHLY REVENUE	ANNUAL REVENUE
Current traffic	100,000	1.00%	$50	$50,000	$600,000
0%	100,000	1.25%	$50	$62,500	$750,000
0%	100,000	1.50%	$50	$75,000	$900,000
0%	100,000	1.75%	$50	$87,500	$1,050,000

You've seen how increasing traffic via SEO efforts and web usability, as separate initiatives, gives us a lift in revenue. But what about when you use them in concert to implement a holistic search usability program?

Table 7.3 shows the potential gain from increasing monthly unique visits and page view to conversion ratio together. Looking at the most optimistic view of increasing traffic by 15 percent to 115,000 monthly unique visits and page view to conversion ratio of .75 percent from 1.00 percent to 1.75 percent, you see an increase of $607,500 in annual revenue as compared to our baseline of $600,000 ($1,207,500 – $600,000). In the more conservative scenario of increasing traffic by 5 percent to 105,000 monthly unique visits and page view to conversion ratio of .25 percent from 1.00 percent to 1.25 percent, you see an increase of $187,500 ($787,500 – $600,000) in annual revenue as compared to the baseline of $600,000.

TABLE 7.3 Products and services model with holistic approach of both usability and SEO efforts

CURRENT AND PROSPECTIVE TRAFFIC	MONTHLY UNIQUE VISITS	PAGE VIEW TO CONVERSION RATIO	AVERAGE PURCHASE	MONTHLY REVENUE	ANNUAL REVENUE
Current traffic	100,000	1.00%	$50	$50,000	$600,000
Plus 5%	105,000	1.25%	$50	$65,625	$787,500
Plus 10%	110,000	1.50%	$50	$82,500	$990,000
Plus 15%	115,000	1.75%	$50	$100,625	$1,207,500

The best scenario is to increase quantity of SEO traffic and improve the search usability of your website. Not all websites will be able to scale results as dramatically as Tables 7.1, 7.2, and 7.3 illustrate. Websites that have more modest traffic will still see results from implementing a holistic search usability initiative, but it will take longer to realize the ROI.

In many cases, when you improve both SEO and web usability you achieve a multiplicative effect that compounds benefits instead of an additive effect. In other words, search usability is often greater than the sum of its parts.

Selling Ads with Search Usability

Online ads come in various shapes, sizes, and technologies. One thing they have in common is the advertising model used by many news and information websites. The advertising model is CPM (cost-per-thousand) in which the cost of advertising is based on the number of times an ad loads on a web page. We'll take a look at some examples based on a CPM of $1 to illustrate our how dramatic your results can be at a low CPM. Depending on the site, the typical CPM can be well over $1.

Let's take a look at how to leverage search usability to contribute to the bottom line for websites with "products and services" advertising models to sell online ads. Let's first take a look at the factors that will help determine the ROI of our search usability investment.

For example, to calculate the monthly revenue in the selling ads with the search usability model you use the formula:

(Monthly page views × Average page views) × CPM = Monthly revenue

- **Page views:** A page view, or page impression, is when a single web page loads in a browser as a result of a user clicking a link or a user typing a URL directly into the browser address bar.

- **Average page views:** Page views are commonly thought of in terms of average page views per visitor. Average page views are the average number of pages a user views during a website session on a given website.

- **CPM:** CPM, or cost-per-thousand, is an advertising model in which an advertiser is charged per thousand times their ad loads on a page. The M in CPM represents the Roman numeral for 1,000.

- **Monthly revenue:** Monthly revenue is the result of multiplying our predefined quantities:

  (Monthly page views × Average page views) × CPM =
  Monthly revenue

When you plug in the values of 100,000 monthly unique page views, a 2.25 average page view, and a $1 CPM, the monthly revenue looks like this:

$$(100,000 \times 2.25) \times \$1 = \$225,000$$

- **Annual revenue:** You generate annual revenue by multiplying the monthly revenue by 12.

Let's take a look at what you can expect from search usability in relation to ROI now that you know the factors that make up your CPM model. **Table 7.4** shows the annual revenue results for an information website by increasing page views via SEO efforts.

TABLE 7.4 CPM model with increased annual revenue via SEO efforts

CURRENT AND PROSPECTIVE TRAFFIC	MONTHLY UNIQUE PAGE VIEWS	AVERAGE PAGE VIEWS	CPM	MONTHLY REVENUE	ANNUAL REVENUE
Current traffic	100,000	2.25	$1	$225,000	$2,700,000
Plus 5%	105,000	2.25	$1	$236,250	$2,835,000
Plus 10%	110,000	2.25	$1	$247,500	$2,970,000
Plus 15%	115,000	2.25	$1	$258,750	$3,105,000

Table 7.4 shows us an increase in annual revenue by increasing the number of pages viewed via SEO efforts. The only factor that changes in Table 7.4 is the monthly page views. Note the increase in annual revenue by increasing the monthly page views by 5, 10, and 15 percent. Even at a CPM of $1 the increase in the annual revenue is $405,000 ($3,105,000 – $2,700,000) between current traffic and a traffic increased by 15 percent.

Using the same model, let's take a look at the annual results when you don't increase the SEO traffic but increase the average page views by improving the search usability of the website.

In **Table 7.5**, the only variable that changes is the average page views. Using an incremental gain of .25 page views, you see an increase of $900,000 ($3,600,000 – $2,700,000) in annual revenue when comparing 2.25 average page views to 3.00 average page views.

TABLE 7.5 CPM model with increased average page view via search usability

CURRENT AND PROSPECTIVE TRAFFIC	MONTHLY UNIQUE PAGE VIEWS	AVERAGE PAGE VIEWS	CPM	REVENUE FOR TRAFFIC	ANNUAL REVENUE
Current traffic	100,000	2.25	$1	$225,000	$2,700,000
0%	100,000	2.50	$1	$250,000	$3,000,000
0%	100,000	2.75	$1	$275,000	$3,300,000
0%	100,000	3.00	$1	$300,000	$3,600,000

The more difficult your site is to navigate and locate relevant information the easier it will be to increase average page views via search usability. Sites with better information architecture and stronger scents of information might find themselves fighting for that additional page view from users, while other sites might see a relatively quick increase in page views due to the poor information scent their site had before implementing search usability. Looking at the dramatic increase in annual revenue, it's difficult to argue against fighting for that additional page view no matter what your situation is.

Table 7.5 assumes that there is no increase in the monthly unique visits from SEO efforts, but rather the increase in annual revenue is 100 percent attributable to increasing the average page view by improving the search usability. Items that could have contributed to the boost in average page view include:

- Improving the findability of content by improving the scent of information

- Featuring related links on content pages to keep users engaged

- Improving the categorization of content

- Improving the readability of your content with headers that more accurately reflect your content

- Improving the scanability of your content with bullets and numbered lists

Now, let's take a look at **Table 7.6** to see the increase of annual revenue in a CPM advertising model when you use a holistic approach to search usability and SEO.

TABLE 7.6 CPM model with holistic approach of SEO efforts and search usability efforts

CURRENT AND PROSPECTIVE TRAFFIC	MONTHLY UNIQUE PAGE VIEWS	AVERAGE PAGE VIEWS	CPM	REVENUE FOR TRAFFIC	ANNUAL REVENUE
Current traffic	100,000	2.25	$1	$225,000	$2,700,000
Plus 5%	105,000	2.50	$1	$262,500	$3,150,000
Plus 10%	110,000	2.75	$1	$302,500	$3,630,000
Plus 15%	115,000	3.00	$1	$345,000	$4,140,000

Table 7.6 shows the potential increase in annual revenue from increasing *both* monthly page views and average page views. In the most optimistic view shown on the last line of Table 7.6 (which includes a 15 percent increase in SEO traffic to 115,000 monthly unique visits and increased average page views of .75 from 2.25 to 3.00), you see an increase

of $1,440,000 ($2,700,000 – $4,140,000) in annual revenue as compared to the baseline on the first row. The more conservative scenario of increasing traffic by 5 percent to 105,000 monthly unique visits and an average page view of 2.50 shows an increase of $450,000 ($3,150,000 – $2,700,000) in annual revenue when compared to the baseline in the first line.

If users can't find what they are looking for they will eventually seek out another source for information.

If your advertising model is based on page views and CPM, you might think pogo-sticking could be beneficial for your advertising model because it can increase page views and you could charge more for advertising. Pogo-sticking may increase page views, but any financial rewards accumulated as a result would only be temporary. The more your site's organization makes users pogo-stick, the more difficult it will be for users to find what they're looking for. If users can't find what they are looking for they will eventually seek another source for information. Additionally, website owners typically don't link to sites they find frustrating to navigate, so naturally occurring inbound links will become less frequent and inbound links will become more difficult to acquire.

Some of the user goals that are essential to news and information websites include being able to find important information quickly and easily. You can increase page views and resulting revenue by increasing accessibility to these items by improving the scent of information.

Supporting Existing Products and Services

The average company loses 10 percent of its customers every year. For every customer a company loses, it needs to acquire a new customer just to maintain customer numbers. The cost to acquire a new customer can be upwards of five times greater or even more than retaining a current customer.

Additionally, companies have a better chance of *cross-selling* to an existing customer than to a former customer or to someone to whom they have never sold before. Therefore, it's a profitable strategy to keep as much of your current customer base as possible.

In an attempt to keep costs down and reduce the number of customers who "walk out" each year, companies implement customer retention programs. One customer retention strategy is to offer superior support on existing products and services to prevent losing customers to competitors.

NOTE *Cross-selling* is the act of selling an additional product or service to an existing or interested customer. An example of a cross-sell on the web would be a website that sells sneakers and features a call-out for "socks that go great with these sneakers." Another common cross-sell technique used on the on web is when websites say, "People who bought product X also bought product Y."

As you know from being a consumer yourself, support comes in variety of forms. Phone and online are the primary ways you get customer support. Phone support can cost a company a lot of money as the more calls that come in to a call center the more people are needed to answer those calls. This is also true with click to call and click to chat technologies, as these technologies require human resources. A website, however, can serve multiple service requests at any time, day or night. The more a customer's support is resolved online the less need there is to staff a call center or customer service department. That could mean significant savings for a company's bottom line. Search usability efforts can help control operational expenses by reducing the number of phone calls that customer service receives.

Let's take a look at the factors that determine the ROI of search usability investment to lower operational costs of supporting existing products and services.

For example, to calculate the monthly cost of calls with the search usability model you use the formula:

(Monthly unique visits × Calls to customer service ratio) ×
(Customer service hourly rate × handle time) = Monthly cost of calls

TIP You can determine the visit to call ratio of your site by putting a unique customer service or call center number on the website. Track the number of calls that come in through the unique number and compare them to the visits your website is receiving to determine your visit to call ratio.

- **Calls to customer service ratio:** This is the ratio of the number of site visits to calls an e-commerce website can expect to receive. A reasonable ratio is 15 percent, based on our experience.

- **Customer service hourly rate:** An hourly rate, such as $50, is the cost of providing the customer service. Depending on your business model, your customer service might be higher or lower. Adjust the dollar amount as necessary. We've assumed that the average handle time (AHT) with a customer is a half hour. The half hour handle time (.5) is baked into the formula.

- **Monthly cost of calls:** Monthly cost of calls is the result of multiplying predefined quantities:

NOTE Call centers and customer service centers use *average handle time (AHT)* as a metric to measure the average duration of a transaction made over the phone. AHT includes hold time, talk time, and necessary tasks that follow the transaction. AHT is a driving metric when projecting call center staffing levels.

(Monthly unique visits × Calls to customer service ratio) ×
(Customer service hourly rate × handle time) = Monthly cost of calls

When you plug in the values of 100,000 monthly unique visits, 15 percent calls to customer service, an hourly rate of $50, and an AHT of .5, the monthly cost of a call looks like this

(100,000 × 15%) × ($50 × .5) = $375,000

- **Annual cost of calls:** You generate annual cost of calls by multiplying the monthly cost of calls by 12.

Let's take a look in **Table 7.7** at how search usability can lower customer service expenses by reducing phone support. This could apply to an e-commerce site, a personal banking site, or just about any other website that costs the business more to have a customer or prospect pick up the phone than it does to have them self-support online.

TABLE 7.7 Improving SEO traffic increases the customer support costs

CURRENT AND PROSPECTIVE TRAFFIC	MONTHLY UNIQUE VISITS	CALLS TO CUSTOMER SERVICE	CUSTOMER SERVICE HOURLY RATE	MONTHLY COST OF CALLS	ANNUAL COST OF CALLS
Current traffic	100,000	15%	$50	$375,000	$4,500,000
Plus 5%	105,000	15%	$50	$393,750	$4,725,000
Plus 10%	110,000	15%	$50	$412,500	$4,950,000
Plus 15%	115,000	15%	$50	$431,250	$5,175,000

Looking at Table 7.7, you see that increasing traffic to a website also increases the customer service operational costs (or customer support department costs). SEO efforts might be considered a failure despite increasing traffic by 15 percent if the operational costs associated with the increase in traffic don't outweigh the monetary benefits of our SEO. To put it another way, if every additional user that SEO drives to the site is worth an average of $1 of revenue but costs the business an average of $2 in operational expenses, SEO might be considered a failure due to the uncalculated associated operational costs to your client. This is something site owners typically don't track or anticipate.

SEO results might result in expenses the business didn't account for or isn't interested in supporting. Some of these expenses might include operational expenses, added head count in the call center or customer service department, and associated management costs needed to support the additional calls despite the positive revenue stream.

The question then is how do we use search usability to lower operational costs to support the bottom line? The first step is finding out what information users are trying to locate that they can't find online or simply isn't available online. Talk to customer service managers, interview customer service representatives, and listen in on customer support calls to discover what type of website content would be beneficial to users.

> **TIP** To lower incoming phone calls, put support information on areas of the site where you can add help content under FAQs, on glossary pages, and "how to" pages.

Let's take a look at the annual cost of calls when you improve search usability. **Table 7.8** uses an incremental decrease of .25 percent in calls to customer service. Note the effect it has on the annual cost of calls.

TABLE 7.8 Increasing search usability sufficiency by .25% lowers operational costs

CURRENT AND PROSPECTIVE TRAFFIC	MONTHLY UNIQUE VISITS	CALLS TO CUSTOMER SERVICE	CUSTOMER SERVICE HOURLY RATE	MONTHLY COST OF CALLS	ANNUAL COST OF CALLS
Current traffic	100,000	15.00%	$50	$375,000	$4,500,000
	100,000	14.75%	$50	$368,750	$4,425,000
	100,000	14.50%	$50	$362,500	$4,350,000
	100,000	14.25%	$50	$356,250	$4,275,000

Table 7.8 assumes that there is no increase in monthly unique visits, but rather an improvement in search usability that results in a modest .75 percent decrease in calls to customer service from 15 percent to 14.25 percent as shown in the most optimistic scenario shown in the last line of Table 7.8. The decrease in call volume of .75 percent saved the company $225,000 ($4,500,000 – $4,275,000) annually when you compare the most optimistic scenario located on the last line with the baseline located on the first line.

Table 7.9 shows what happens when you increase SEO traffic and reduce call volume. It's not as cut and dried as the previous models because in this case; instead of SEO and usability working in concert, they are actually working against each other from an ROI perspective. The more traffic you drive, the greater your operational costs. The better your search usability, the lower your operational expenses. The best strategy for increasing revenue is to increase traffic and efficiency by increasing both search and usability efforts. We refer to this as *search usability*. This model shows a correlation between the increase in the annual cost of calls and increase in traffic despite the decrease of calls to customer service. The annual cost of calls will vary based on the values used to generate that dollar amount.

TABLE 7.9 Increased SEO traffic and reduced customer service calls

CURRENT AND PROSPECTIVE TRAFFIC	MONTHLY UNIQUE VISITS	CALLS TO CUSTOMER SERVICE	CUSTOMER SERVICE HOURLY RATE	MONTHLY COST OF CALLS	ANNUAL COST OF CALLS
Current traffic	100,000	15.00%	$50	$375,000	$4,500,000
Plus 5%	105,000	14.75%	$50	$387,188	$4,646,250
Plus 10%	110,000	14.50%	$50	$398,750	$4,785,000
Plus 15%	115,000	14.25%	$50	$409,688	$4,916,250

You might find that an increase in traffic yields operating expenses that your search usability can't lower to a desired cost. On the other hand, your search usability might lower your operating expenses and/or cost-per-conversion to a level that allows for extra money in one budget to be used to increase traffic through other search engine marketing initiatives such as pay-per-click.

■ SEARCH USABILITY FOR EMPLOYEE INTRANETS

Intranets are probably the furthest thing from most SEO's minds as intranets have nothing to do with commercial search engines. Intranets do, however, have everything to do with website users and the amount of time they spend completing tasks on the site like looking up a colleague's phone extension or a change of address form for human resources. Such actions make intranets a prime candidate for search usability.

NOTE Every minute that employees spend trying to navigate a clumsy interface is a minute spent away from work that contributes to the bottom line.

Intranets are frequently thrown together as side projects. As long as users can log in to them, intranets are typically considered a success. What is usually not considered is the lost time employees spend trying to use the haphazardly constructed website. Let's see how you can use search usability to lower operating expenses by implementing search usability into the company intranet.

TIP In the absence of actual data, many managers just double the average salary of a given group of workers to obtain the "loaded labor rate."

There is much that goes into building an intranet other than lowering time on task. This is not the book for designing intranets. However, we wanted to show the correlation between the ease of use in finding information on an intranet and lowing business expenses.

For example, to calculate the monthly cost of intranet use by increasing employee efficiency you use the formula:

(Number of employees × Hours of intranet usage per month) ×
Average hourly rate = Monthly cost of intranet use

- **Number of employees:** We used 100 for the number of employees in this model. An organization smaller than 100 employees probably wouldn't get the cost/benefit out of having an intranet. An exception would be a company that has a large portion of its employees working remotely who don't have easy access to network drives or company documents.

- **Hours of intranet usage per month:** We begin our assumption at one hour.

- **Average hourly rate:** This is the average hourly rate of an employee. Your average hourly rate of an employee might be different depending on your business model.

■ **Monthly cost of intranet use:** Monthly cost of intranet use is the result of multiplying predefined quantities.

(Number of employees × Hours of intranet usage per month) × Average hourly rate = Monthly cost of intranet use

When you plug in the values of 100 employees, 1 hour of use, and $80 as the average hourly rate, the monthly cost looks like this:

$$(100 \times 1)\, 80 = \$8,000$$

■ **Annual cost of intranet use:** You generate annual cost of intranet use by multiplying the monthly cost of intranet use by 12.

Table 7.10 shows how increasing the efficiency of employee intranet use can quickly begin lowering operational costs by increasing the efficiency of employees.

TABLE 7.10 Decreasing cost by increasing employee efficiency

NUMBER OF EMPLOYEES	INTRANET USAGE PER MONTH (HRS)	AVERAGE HOURLY RATE	MONTHLY COST OF INTRANET USE	ANNUAL COST OF INTRANET USE	ANNUAL REVENUE
100	1.00	$80	$8,000	$96,000	$2,700,000
100	0.75	$80	$6,000	$72,000	$2,835,000
100	0.50	$80	$4,000	$48,000	$2,970,000
100	0.25	$80	$2,000	$24,000	$3,105,000

Table 7.10 is an illustration of the old adage "time is money." By making information easier to find on the company intranet, you reduce the time employees lose navigating the intranet and give them back time that can be better spent contributing to the bottom line.

■ COMMON SEARCH USABILITY GOALS

We just took a look at some of the most common primary goals based on the type of site. Now, let's take a look at common search usability goals that are shared by all types of websites.

Top SERP Rankings

We need to rethink the perception of number one SERP rankings.

Number one rankings are only valuable if they lead users from the SERPs to users' desired content on your website, resulting in an action that directly or indirectly contributes to your business's bottom line.

NOTE Number one SERP rankings can actually hurt a company's reputation if users can't find the information they are looking for on a SERP listing. If users can't find their desired information on your site, the number one ranking contributes to a poor user experience and equates to a bad brand experience, which devalues the brand.

Only when you can tie your SERP listings back to conversions will the true value of your SEO efforts be understood.

We need to rethink the perception of number one SERP rankings.

Imagine you are a client considering hiring one of a couple SEO firms. Firm A shows results that detail they achieved page one rankings for 10 very competitive terms in a matter of six months, resulting in a 25 percent increase in natural traffic.

Firm B showed similar increases in natural traffic but also reports that the increase of traffic contributed to over $150,000 in new sales in six months and 90 percent of those purchases were by new visitors. Of those new visitors, 30 percent returned to make another purchase on the site, while an additional 10 percent joined the email list. Additionally, based on historical client data that Firm B was able to communicate, we can count on 3 purchases averaging $65 over a period of 12 months from 15 percent of email subscribers.

> **Note** A *conversion* might be buying a product or downloading a whitepaper. It might also be getting users to a certain type of page so you can charge more for advertising revenue. You'll need to define what a conversion is for your business.

Most companies would prefer to hire Firm B due to their understanding of ROI and accountability.

Your ability to track your results might be limited by technology such as web analytics or by marketing's ability track efforts.

SEOs should work with marketing to develop metrics that will help tie SEO efforts to conversions. This communicates to marketing professionals that SEOs are making an attempt to be financially accountable for their actions.

> **Tip** Be conservative with your marketing goals. It's better to under-promise and over-deliver than over-promise and under-deliver.

Bounce Rates

A *bounce* happens when a user arrives on your website and leaves after viewing only one page. The act of the user leaving is the bounce. If 100 users land on page A and 40 of them abandon the site without navigating to another page, page A would have a bounce rate of 40 percent.

There's a concern among SEOs as to how or if commercial search engines account for bounce rates. Search engines do consider bounce rates in their algorithms. Exactly how much weight the search engines give bounce rate is unknown. Regardless, when measuring your website's bounce rates, gathering user feedback is more important than chasing search engine algorithms. We'll address gathering user feedback in Chapter 9, "How to Improve Your Website's Search Usability."

Bounce rate alone may not tell the whole story. A high bounce rate may indicate a poor user experience, or to the contrary that your users are finding what they are looking for and can quickly move on from your site.

Examples of a positive bounce rate for an e-commerce site include users who are comparison shopping. Users can compare the prices of the same pair of shoes from three different sites within minutes and return later to complete a purchase. In this case of comparison shopping, the bounce rate is high but the users found exactly what they were looking for in a very short amount of time.

Other tasks that contribute to a positive high bounce rate include ones that can be accomplished quickly, such as locating a phone number, finding the location of a business, and other tasks that can be completed from an entry page.

A negative bounce will happen when your SERP listing doesn't match the content of its respective page or your users' intent or if your users can't find the information they are looking for. You'll receive a negative bounce when your scent of information is weak, if users don't feel like they have arrived at the right page for their query, or they don't find links to their desired content from the entry page.

Instead of trying to lower or increase a bounce rate per se, look to improve (increase or decrease) a bounce rate based on your users' goals. You can improve your overall bounce rates by making your SERP listings accurately reflect their respective page content. The more relevant your content is to your users' intent, the better your bounce rate will be, be it higher for pages that immediately help users complete a task like finding a phone number, or lower for pages like category pages that lead users to sought-after information.

Time-on-Site and Page Views

Time-on-site is a web analytic metric that measures the total time a user spends on a website. *Page views* are the number of pages a user navigates to during his time on a website.

Many web professionals tend to think the more time-on-site and the more page views, the better their website is performing. But just like bounce rate, our interpretation of the time-on-site and page view numbers might be wrong.

You don't know the reason one user spent two minutes on your website viewing three pages and another spent three minutes on your website viewing five pages. Web analytics data is just that: data. The numbers don't tell you why users acted they way they did. You might like to think that your content is engaging your users and that's why they are spending the amount of time on our site viewing the number pages they are viewing. However, the opposite might be true. A longer time-on-site and more page views per visitor might indicate users pogo-sticking on your site, not being able to locate their desired information, and as a result generating a longer time-on-site than desired.

Conversely, less time-on-site and fewer page views are frequently seen as indicators of a website not engaging users. But this might also be false if users are finding exactly what they are looking for and can leave the site satisfied after only spending 30 seconds and two page views on the site.

The problem is that time-on-site and page views, like bounce rate, only give enough information for us to speculate why users are spending the time on the site. If you really want to understand the behavior behind time-on-site and page views, you need to perform usability testing, which is covered in Chapter 9. Only then will you begin to understand the "why" behind the numbers.

> **NOTE** We'll look at how to determine the why in Chapter 9, "How to Improve Your Website's Search Usability."

■ CONCLUSION

Here are the key points of this chapter:

- Businesses make money by increasing revenue or lowering operating expenses. Search usability can be used to support both of these objectives.

- Use realistic numbers when developing your search usability models. Miscalculations in monthly estimates will be multiplied 12 fold in your annual results.

- It's best to use historical data when developing your search usability models. If you don't have historical data, use third-party data if available or SWAG it.

- The most important factor in developing your models is setting client and management expectations correctly. If necessary, use a range of numbers to project your results.

- The more difficult it is to navigate and find information on your website, the greater the ROI you can achieve by improving your search usability.

- Many businesses lose 10 percent of their customers each year. Search usability can reduce customer attrition by making product and support information more findable on the website.

- Search usability can increase employee productivity by making intranet content more findable.

- A number one SERP ranking might be hurting your company's reputation if users can't find their desired content after clicking it.

- Bounce rates can be easily misinterpreted. A high bounce rate might mean users found what they were looking for on a single page and were able to move on from your site.

- Time-on-site and page views, like bounce rates, can be easily misinterpreted. A longer time-on-site doesn't mean a better user experience. It could mean that issuers are trying harder to find their desired content. The same is true of page views.

- Conduct usability testing to understand the behavior that drives web analytic data such as bounce rates, time-on-site, and page views.

CHAPTER 8

SEARCH USABILITY IS EVERYONE'S JOB

As a search professional, you have a unique opportunity to touch everyone who works on or has interest in a website. It is in your best interest to educate everyone so they can help you accomplish your search usability goals. Having access to many of the players such as writers, developers, marketers, and designers also makes you a prime candidate to infuse search usability into the website.

We are not suggesting that one search professional can change an entire corporate culture overnight. That would be a delusion. But you can have big impact. This chapter introduces you to the stakeholders in your site's search visibility and what you need to know about each one's perspective.

■ THE HOLE IN THE FENCE: A STORY ABOUT PERSPECTIVE

Jimmy used to watch baseball games through a 2-inch hole in the fence near third base. He would watch a man, standing next to a base, looking straight ahead for about a half hour and then suddenly run off, only to be replaced by someone else who did the same thing. The only difference between the men was that they dressed a little differently.

Every once in a while, someone would run by and stop on the base, and then after a few minutes run out of view. The runner never did stay very long.

Occasionally, the baseman would catch a ball and throw the ball. Sometimes Jimmy would hear the loud roar of a crowd.

Jimmy's perspective on a baseball game was limited by the view he had through the hole in the fence (**Figure 8.1**).

FIGURE 8.1 Jimmy's limited perspective of a baseball game.

©Toonclipart.com

How is Jimmy's perspective on baseball similar to building websites? The greater perspective you have about the players involved, the better you can address business interests, user needs, and the search usability of your website.

■ IT TAKES A VILLAGE TO BUILD FOR SEARCH USABILITY

Many skills contribute to designing for search usability. Each skill is vital to designing *findable* content and a usable interface.

Everyone who is part of the process has the ability to affect search usability positively or negatively. The following sections describe some of the roles that people play in an organization. You may know these roles by different names; the labels aren't as important as the influence each role has on search usability. You'll know who's responsible for what in your organization when you see it. Here's what you need to know about how each affects your site's search usability.

Some web professionals may fill more than one of the following roles in their day-to-day job. They might be a graphic artist and a copywriter. Or they might be an information architect and a usability professional. For the sake of clarity, we will segment out the roles and examine how the skills associated with each role affect search usability. Let's look at how graphic designers, copywriters, marketing communications specialists, usability professionals, management, market researchers, information techs (IT), and information architects (IA) affect a website's search usability.

Graphic Designers and Search Usability

Graphic designers make web pages look attractive and inviting. They are also responsible for presenting data clearly, creating consistent graphic styles, and visually communicating functionality. The choices graphic designers make are critical to search usability as their visual executions affect how users scan, read, and browse web pages.

Graphic design techniques to get users' attention

Graphic design techniques will either attempt to get users' attention or allow a page element to fade into the background. The more aggressive the technique, the more likely it is to grab users' attention—and the less attention users will give to other elements on that page.

The choices graphic designers make are critical to search usability as their visual executions affect how users scan, read, and browse web pages.

Not everything can be the most important thing

We have all seen pages where it looks like every element is screaming for attention.

Everything cannot be the most important thing on the web page. Home pages are usually the biggest casualty of the "everything is important" disease. This line of thinking also finds its way into subpages.

By making everything look equally important, the message you are sending to users is that that nothing is important, which is the exact opposite of what you want. Additionally, the resulting web page often looks cluttered, which can irritate and confuse site visitors.

Everything cannot be the most important thing on the web page.

Miscommunication is only the beginning of your problems. If you do not create a visual hierarchy, users cannot locate what they came to your site to find. Many will abandon your site and go to your competitors' sites.

How to create a visual hierarchy for search usability

As a guideline, it's best to be conservative when designing to get users' attention. Start with less aggressive techniques and work your way up to stronger ones. You can monitor how your efforts change user behavior by looking at your site analytics and by getting user feedback with usability testing.

Remember, the following are general guidelines, not absolutes.

Bold, underlined, and colored text

Using bold, underlining, and different-colored text are subtle techniques that grab the users' attention. These techniques work well in the body of a page and make for easy scanning of copy, links, and subheads.

You can draw users' attention to keywords that keep them engaged by bolding, underlining, and varying text colors. Consistently feeding users the scent of information will increase how much time they spend on your site and increase the page view count.

One of the most common mistakes by graphic designers on web pages is not letting site visitors know what text is clickable and what is not. In the sample on the left in **Figure 8.2**, which text is clickable? Is it the word *download?* Is it the words *free white paper?* Is it the phrase *How to Maximize Your Email Campaigns?* In fact, the text does not look clickable at all. In the sample on the right, the clickable text is much clearer.

Remember, users determine the text they will click before they move their mouse.

> Download our free white paper about "How to Maximize Your Email Campaigns."

> Download our <u>free white paper</u> about "How to Maximize Your Email Campaigns."

FIGURE 8.2 Which example clearly tells users what text is clickable?

Test to see how implementing bolding, underlining, or different colors increases or decreases time on site and average page views.

Graphics

Using well-designed graphics can grab users' attention. Your eyes are naturally drawn to objects that look nice. Hollywood knows this. When was the last time you saw a movie filled with plain-looking people? Plain-looking people movies do not sell. Pretty people movies? They sell.

The same is true on the web. Graphics, if they are done well, look more visually appealing than HTML and grab your attention faster than bolding, underlining, or color variations. Your eyes naturally go from areas of heavy color concentration to lighter color concentration.

Sometimes, users click graphic images more than they click text, and vice versa. A savvy graphic designer knows when it is appropriate to use graphic images only, text only, or a combination of text and graphics to provide the strongest information scent and the best conversions.

In **Figure 8.3** and **Figure 8.4**, a simple change from text to a graphic image results in a much higher click-through and conversion rate.

NOTE Save underlining for links. Some sites underline and add color. Some only underline links in the body of the page. Regular users are more likely to learn the conventions than users who only go to a site once or twice. Still, if you want users to be certain that text is a link, underline the text.

FIGURE 8.3 The call to action <u>Compare Prices</u> in this camera ad is formatted as a simple text link.

FIGURES 8.4 By changing the <u>Compare Prices</u> link to a graphic image and making it stand out with a background color and rounded corners, more users will respond to the desired call to action.

Sound and motion

Have you ever received a musical birthday card—the kind that plays a happy birthday jingle when you open it? You do not even notice how much the enclosed check is for. You're too busy listening to the music.

Sound and motion grab your attention on a web page as quickly as a catchy little jingle from a birthday card does. If you really want to get your users' attention, pull out all the stops and use a Flash movie with sound. Because of the attention they demand, both sound and motion communicate to users that they are at the top of your hierarchy.

A word of caution, however: If you are going to use sound, give users explicit control of the volume and ability to turn it off. Better yet, default the sound to off and let users turn the sound on at their discretion. Sound blaring out from the speakers generally annoys users and just might embarrass them at work.

If you are going to use Flash, be sure the technology promotes your message and doesn't detract from it. Animation, when used appropriately, will attract users to take your call to action. It can also help users achieve their goals. However, if animation distracts users from completing their goals, then it will irritate them and often cause them to leave the site.

Additionally, Flash is not a favorite with the commercial web search engines. Even though they can crawl Flash, most web pages that tend to rank well over time are not built completely in Flash.

Web Copywriters and Search Usability

You do not read information on the web the same way you do in print. Web users primarily scan copy, look for trigger keywords, and click the graphics or text that carries the scent of information for content that strikes their interest.

You read, in the traditional sense, after you find detailed information that matches a query and want to know more about a topic.

Your copy either encourages users to continue on to deeper pages of your site, or the copy confuses them and they use the back button to return to the SERP to refine their query.

Don't let your copy lose the scent of information

Site visitors use copy cues and links on the web to navigate the same way drivers use street signs to navigate on the road. If you do not provide the right cues in your web copy, users lose the scent of information and get lost just like drivers get lost if there are no street signs to follow or if the street signs are poorly labeled.

Let's take it from the driver's point of view. Imagine you are driving in unfamiliar territory. You have no global positioning system (GPS), Google Maps, or access to directions of any kind. You are going to have to drive on local roads and major highways to reach your destination, and you depend on street signs to guide you.

It would be helpful if the local roads had signs that prompted you when you needed to make a turn, reading "This way to your destination" with an arrow pointing. Think of these prompting signs as the equivalent to hyperlinks on your website pages and your listing in the SERPs.

The road you turn down should confirm you made the correct turn by providing a confirmation sign. It should read "This way to your destination" with an arrow that now points straight ahead. Think of these confirmation signs as the equivalent of headers that confirm you landed on the right page from a link or a subhead that confirms you landed on the right section of a page from an *anchor link*.

Think of the highway signs as the equivalent of the overall scent of information. If the driver isn't constantly fed confirmation during his journey, he might get confused and go back a mile or so to try to pick up the scent of information, similar to a user who clicks the back button.

Let's see how to help users get to their destination by providing them a scent of information with copy.

NOTE An HTML *anchor link,* or *jump link*, is a link that takes a user from one part of a page to another part of the same page. It can also be used to take a user to the middle of an HTML page from another page. A common use of an anchor link is the "return to top" link found at the bottom of web pages or sections on a web page.

Identify critical copy areas for including the information scent

Have you ever seen on TV how doctors and nurses communicate with each other during surgery (**Figure 8.5**)? It goes something like this:

- **Doctor:** "Scalpel." (The doctor asks the nurse for a scalpel.)
- **Nurse:** "Scalpel." (The nurse hands the scalpel to the doctor.)
- **Doctor:** "Clamp." (The doctor asks the nurse for a clamp.)
- **Nurse:** "Clamp." (The nurse hands the clamp to the doctor.)

FIGURE 8.5 This is not what the doctor ordered.

On the web, users *ask* for things by clicking words and images. A web page *answers* by displaying information that contextually matches the hyperlinked text or image the user clicked. If the web page doesn't return the appropriate content, the user can get lost.

When users click a link, they need to see the words, or a close variation of the words they clicked below areas of the destination page to help orient themselves.

Take a look at **Figure 8.6** to see how the CIA's careers page satisfies a Google query for *cia careers*.

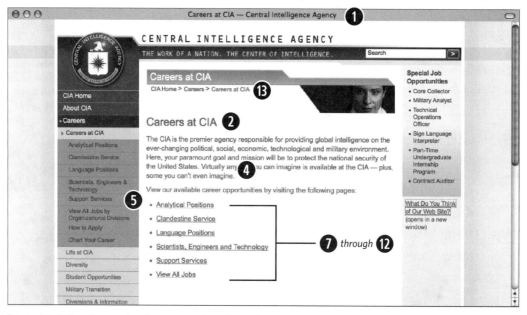

FIGURE 8.6 A Google query for *cia careers* results in the CIA's careers page.

The scent of information also applies to pictures and captions. Photo captions are second only to headlines for readership in newspapers. They are also big attention grabbers on the web. If you are using photos on your pages, be sure to use relevant, informative, precise, and keyword-rich captions.

Putting the appropriate copy in specific parts of the web page will either help users follow the scent of information or hinder them. **Table 8.1** analyzes how the elements on the CIA careers page satisfy the Google query.

Table 8.1 CIA Career page elements.

	PAGE ELEMENT	COPY	COMMENTS
1	Title tag	Careers at CIA–Central Intelligence Agency	Good
2	Heading	Careers at CIA	Good
3	Subheading	*Doesn't exist on this page.*	Adding a subheading using keywords on the page could improve scanning. It might also give commercial search engines additional content to index.
4	Introductory paragraph	View our available career opportunities by visiting the following pages:	Good
5	Bulleted lists	Various job titles (see hypertext links below for more)	Good
6	Captions	*Doesn't exist on this page.*	Adding a picture to the body of the page that complements the content contextually could help users orient themselves. Adding a caption to the picture would give commercial search engines additional content to index.
7	Hypertext link	Analytical Positions	Good
8	Hypertext link	Clandestine Service	Good
9	Hypertext link	Language Positions	Good
10	Hypertext link	Scientists, Engineers and Technology	Good
11	Hypertext link	Support Services	Good
12	Hypertext link	View All Jobs	Good
13	Breadcrumb links	CIA Home > Careers > Careers at CIA	Good
14	Image alternative text	NA	The image near the header is a CSS background image that doesn't allow for alternative text. An image that used keywords in the alternative text would give search engines indexable content and give visually impaired users additional content to help them interpret the page.
15	URL	https://www.cia.gov/careers/jobs/index.html	Good

Reflect the users' language

Reflecting the users' language in the text of a web page in the areas commonly scanned and also on the search engine results pages will help users

- Navigate search engine results pages (SERPs)
- Navigate web pages
- Orient to the page's content

- Accomplish tasks
- Scan more easily
- Reduce pogo-sticking
- Reduce back button use

Copywriters should have access to the results of keyword research to understand what words and phrases users use in their queries when searching on commercial search engines and scanning, foraging, and browsing on your website.

If possible, web copywriters should observe usability tests, talk with focus groups, and have access to other market research noting the words users use to describe products and tasks. Be aware that different users may search differently:

- Younger users may search differently than older users. Research indicates that users over age 60 tend to use links more than search. Also, these users construct less useful search criteria than younger users, thus taking longer to complete the task, or failing altogether.
- Users with more subject matter experience may use different words to search than users with less.
- Users from one region may search differently than users from another region. For example, here are three different names for what is essentially carbonated sugar water:
  - *Pop* in the Midwestern area of the United States
  - *Soft drink* in Australia
  - *Soda* in New Jersey

Format copy for search usability

Formatting copy is as important to search usability as the keywords used in your web copy. Consider the following writing guidelines for search usability:

- Write in a journalistic style using an inverted pyramid with the most important information at the top of the page and above the fold.
- Use short paragraphs, two to three sentences each, similar to newspaper paragraphs. To aid scanning, consider using a header for every two to three short paragraphs, and for every paragraph longer than five to seven sentences.
- Mix paragraphs with long, short, and medium-length sentences. Keep within a 20-word maximum for a sentence.
- Use bullets in lieu of paragraphs to help users scan content.

- Use numbered steps if you are writing instructions, such as recipes for cooking.
- Present information to users in snack sizes. Avoid serving up large portions of text.
- Get to the point with your copy. Avoid using overblown excessive hype.
- Left-hand justify your copy.
- Make body copy hypertext about 7 to 12 words long.

Marketing Communications and Search Usability

Marketing communications professionals know every touch point, including a website, has the potential to build a relationship with customers. This makes marketing communications a prime candidate to help infuse search usability because it can have a big impact on branding.

Bad search usability equals bad brand experience

A poor search usability experience gives you a similar feeling to what you get when you are left on hold listening to "Your call is very important to us. Please hold and your call will be answered in the order in which it was received."

Do you really feel your call is important after you have been on hold for 10 minutes? No.

This type of experience devalues the brand.

Users feel the same way about poor website experiences. The more users are forced to muddle through your website not finding what they are looking for, the more your website communicates a negative brand experience.

Four user behaviors to tip you off that your website might be degrading your brand

User behaviors that can tip you off that your site is degrading your brand are

- Back button use
- Pogo-sticking
- Site search use
- Site maps (wayfinder) use

NOTE Jared Spool refers to the back button as the "button of doom."

Each of these behaviors communicates that users can't find what they are looking for by using the primary navigation. If you discover your users exhibiting these behaviors, there's a good chance that your information architecture doesn't make sense or your website's scent of information is not strong enough.

NOTE *Brand equity* refers to the value a consumer places on your brand.

A website that doesn't help users find what they are looking for is a website that devalues your brand equity—brand equity that you have built up through the years with thousands or millions of dollars spent on radio, billboards, TV, pay-per-click advertising, and direct mail.

In addition to devaluing branding, back button use, pogo-sticking, and the use of supplemental navigation items like site search and site maps contribute significantly to decreased conversions.

NOTE Learn more about back button use, pogo-sticking, and site search behavior from Jared Spools' July 2008 webinar entitled "The Scent of a Web Page: The Five Types of Navigation Pages" located in the virtual seminar catalog: www.uie.com/events/ virtual_seminars/. Jared Spool is the CEO of User Interface Engineering (www.uie.com).

What can you do to improve users' success rate?

By watching some specific areas, you can improve your users' success rate on your site.

Reduce back button use and pogo-sticking

You can reduce back button use and pogo-sticking by improving the scent of information by using keywords consistently throughout key areas of a website such as headers, breadcrumbs, and clearly defined links.

Reduce site searches

The reason site search contributes so heavily to failure is because most searches fail users. Site search design generally does not receive the same attention and budget that other portions of the site get.

aTest your site search. Make sure it is delivering the most helpful content it can to your users during what may be a very vulnerable time on your site.

Create a user-friendly site map

You need to move beyond site maps designed solely to give commercial search engines access to your web pages and work to improve your site maps to better serve users who might be one click away from abandoning.

User-friendly site maps are easy and cheap to build and implement, and you hardly have to change your site other than adding a link to the utility navigation and/or the footer navigation.

A user-friendly site map should provide links to the most important areas of the website. These areas should include a combination of category pages and product or information pages that are critical to accomplishing user and business goals. Links should be annotated to describe what users will find on the respective pages and in subdirectories. The link annotations should also provide keyword-rich content for the search engines to spider.

Smaller websites might be able to get away with providing links to every page on the site. Larger sites might need to limit site maps to the most important pages and/or provide multiple site maps in each major section of the site.

Communicate crisis information

Crises don't happen every day, but when they do they often strike fast and without warning.

Depending on the severity of the crisis you may need to

- Post an announcement on the home page that links to your press release.
- Replace your homepage with a single announcement on your home page.
- Post a press release in the news section of your website.

In the event of a crisis, be sure the press and anyone else interested can find

- What the company has to say about the crisis.
- Who to contact in the event of a crisis. It could be a PR agency or an internal employee.
- Company name, location of the company headquarters, website of the company, and executive team.

The last thing you want is the media finding information about your crisis on someone else's site or blog because you weren't prepared.

Acting fast so the media and your customers can find information on your website can improve your users' experience, your site's search usability, and may actually be an opportunity to build brand trust by proactively making an effort to get the users to their desired content, even if it is about a crisis.

Usability Professionals and Search Usability

Usability professionals keep the users as their focal point when developing a product or service. Usability professionals conduct usability tests to be sure users can use a website effectively, reducing the time it takes to learn an interface and to complete tasks. Usability professionals pick up where search engine optimizers (SEOs) leave off, working to keep users on a site and getting them to their desired information.

In general, web usability professionals do not take into account two key items regarding search usability: querying behavior and keyword research.

Querying—a behavior usability professionals ignore

Many usability professionals start testing from the home page or an interior page. Usability professionals typically don't take into account the querying behavior performed on commercial search engines that brings the majority of users to a site. This is a mistake.

Figure 8.7 shows web analytics data for a particular site. This pie chart shows that the majority of users found the site by entering a query into a commercial search engine. Why would usability professionals not consider the behavior of most of its site visitors?

FIGURE 8.7 Web analytics data clearly shows most site visitors reached a page within this site through a search engine.

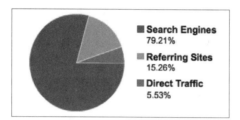

Usability professionals need to look at site analytics to see how users are reaching the site. What they need to look for is

- Percentage of users who find the site via commercial search engines

- Entry pages

- Keywords that brought users to entry pages

- Bounce rates

- Conversions attributed by path

The goal is to determine the type of query used to find a particular page. By understanding the type of query, be it navigational, informational, or transactional, you can better anticipate the intent of the users and give them access to information that is most relevant to their query.

This is where linking among pages of your website becomes critical, as you need to try to address the interests of multiple types of users.

Maximizing an information query

If it is the users' intent is to find information, you should not only provide the information they seek, but provide access to additional relevant information to keep users on the site. Other types of information pages include

- Frequently Asked Questions (FAQs), Help, or Customer Service

- Press releases

- Tips pages

For example, as shown in **Figure 8.8**, the National Cancer Institute provides links to various related information from the main Pancreatic Cancer category page, including information on

1. Pancreatic cancer treatments
2. Prevention of pancreatic cancer
3. Screening for pancreatic cancer
4. The page also features "General Cancer Resources" in the right-hand column, which gives access to more general, but still highly relevant, information.

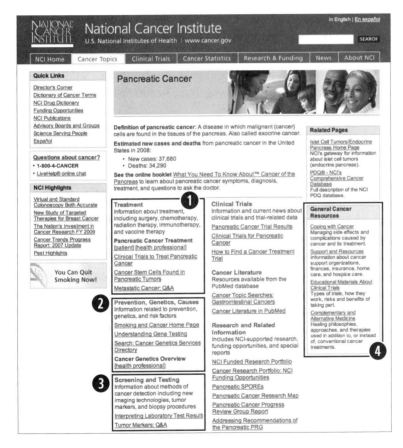

FIGURE 8.8 The category page for Pancreatic Cancer at the National Cancer Institute's website provides strong scents of information that encourage site visitors to continue viewing pages within the Pancreatic Cancer section. Links are reinforced with keyword-focused annotations and relevant hypertext links.

Analyzing the quality of search engine traffic

Traffic from the commercial web search engines is user initiated, prequalified, and task-based. Therefore, users arriving at a site via a search engine should be more interested in your content than users who landed on your website by clicking links out of curiosity from other websites or found your site through social networking websites.

If a good portion of your search engine traffic is bouncing off the page soon after arriving on your website, you may have to take a good look at your entry pages and queries that brought users to your website to find out why users are bouncing off. Web analytics may only tell you half the story. You may have to usability test to get a better idea of why users aren't finding what they are looking for.

Ask these questions:

- **Scent of information.** Are you using the same keywords on your landing page, be it the home page or interior pages, as was displayed in the SERP? And if you are, can users easily find it?

- **User expectations.** Did you meet your users' expectations of content that would be on the web page based on which SERP listing they clicked?

NOTE A/B and multivariate testing are the preferred test methods for comparing two prior months of data. These are sometimes referred to as a *pre-post test* and can be influenced by seasonality, news, and time-sensitive promotions.

You can measure the results of your changes in your web analytics by comparing two prior months of data or running *A/B* or *multivariate* testing to see if you were able to

- Lower bounce rate of your targeted users from this page

- Increase page views for these users (but not at the expense of pogo-sticking)

- Increase conversions attributable to this entry page

Which is it—informational query or transactional query?

It can be difficult to differentiate between informational and transactional queries when looking at web analytics. As a result, you'll need to anticipate multiple mental models depending on the query used to find your web page(s).

In **Figure 8.9**, the data from Google analytics shows some ambiguous keyword phrases that could qualify for either informational or transactional queries.

FIGURE 8.9 Take a look at the keyword phrase *eco-friendly vacation packages.* Was the searcher looking for information about available vacation packages? Or was he looking to book a trip? Is it an informational or transactional query? It's a tough call.

Keyword
1. ecotourism jamaica
2. ecotourism and jamaica
3. jamacian vacations
4. jamaica ecotourism
5. caribbean ecotourism all-inclusive
6. caribbean vacation packages march
7. eco friendly vacation packages
8. eco-friendly all inclusive
9. ecotourism vacation packages

If your information pages are found as a result of transactional queries, make calls to actions easy to find to help users stay on the information scent.

Commercial web search engines are not perfect. For example, sometimes informational pages, such as this category page from the National Cancer Institute website in **Figure 8.10**, appear in search results along with transactional pages. Nevertheless, the main calls to action on this category page are easy to find:

1. The hypertext link to the booklet "What You Need to Know About™ Cancer of the Pancreas" is located in the center of the page, and the link is underlined to indicate that it's clickable.

2. Likewise, if searchers want information about pancreatic cancer treatments, the labels, annotations, and hypertext links are clearly indicated in the "Treatment" section of the page.

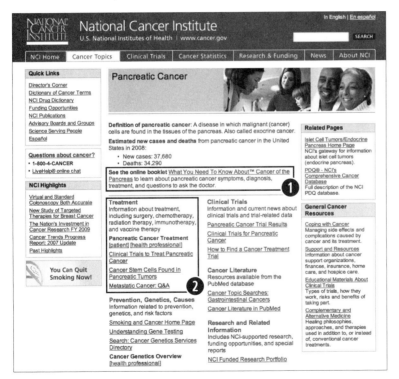

FIGURE 8.10 National Cancer Institute informational page can match a transactional query.

If your transactional pages are being found for informational queries, be sure to give sufficient access to other informational pages. Provide a clear scent of information to related pages that users will find of interest, as shown in **Figure 8.11** on the next page. If this e-commerce site's product page appears in search results for an informational query, it helps guide searchers to other circular saws available on the site.

1. The location breadcrumb link provides both a sense of place and an information scent should searchers wish to view a list of available circular saws.

2. The hierarchical hyperlink in the product details section also guides users to the circular saws subcategory page.

3. The thumbnail photo links and corresponding hypertext links to other product pages provide a very strong, relevant scent of information to specific product pages of interest.

4. The global navigation label guides searchers even further up the site's hierarchy to a main category page.

FIGURE 8.11 This type of product page appropriately accommodates both informational and transactional search engine queries.

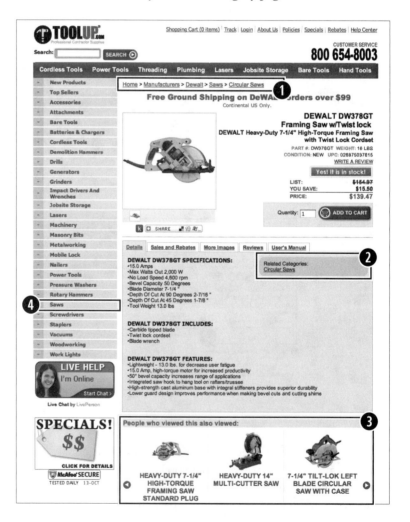

Keyword research—the overlooked user language

The second factor web usability professionals discount is keyword research. Using the users' language is touted in the web usability community through various research methods including one-on-one interviews, focus groups, and surveys, but keyword research is not a widely promoted method.

Web usability professionals should familiarize themselves with the paid and free keyword research tools and other keyword research methods used by search engine optimization professionals.

Using keyword research tools, you'll see the most popular keywords users use to query, keywords usage trends, and variations of keyword phrases users favor.

Some tools that SEO professionals use include Google Adwords Research Tool (free), and Keyword Discovery and WordTracker (both of which have free and paid versions).

TIP Here are a few URLs to help you begin your keyword research: https://adwords.google.com/select/KeywordToolExternal, www.keyworddiscovery.com, and www.wordtracker.com

Early, often, and together

Usability and search professionals should work with each other early and often during the build and launch of a website. If you wait until the end of a project to implement search usability, chances are you going to have to re-engineer part or all of the website. No one likes to hear that their $50,000 website isn't paying the bills.

If you are a usability professional coming into a project, be sure to ask if there is a search professional working on it. Search professionals should ask who is handling the web usability. Sometimes search and usability professionals are working on the same website and don't even know it.

The earlier you bring search usability into your project the more likely your website will be successful.

Management and Search Usability

According to a study published in the journal *Psychological Science*, someone's ability to consider another perspective decreases in proportion to the level of power in a given relationship. This explains why some of us have a difficult time selling to upper management.

Just because management frequently thinks they are right doesn't mean they are. Let's take a look at how management's way of thinking affects search usability.

Management often doesn't manage to ask what's wanted

Have you ever been to a white elephant gift exchange party? A white elephant party is where everyone brings a wrapped unwanted gift they have received and ultimately walks away with someone else's unwanted gift—a gift that's hopefully more desirable than the one they brought.

Many of the crummy gifts that find their way to the white elephant party come from well-intentioned gift-givers, such as family or close friends. People who would swear they know whom they are buying for.

So, why so many crummy gifts? Crummy gifts happen when people incorrectly or inaccurately assume the preferences of others. Sure, a surprise is always nice, but a gift we are sure to like beats a bad surprise any day of the week (**Figure 8.12**).

Figure 8.12 They could have at least asked me what I wanted instead of guessing...

Poor search usability is very similar to receiving a crummy gift. The difference is that your users don't politely smile and tell you they love your gift and rewrap it in hopes of later unloading it on someone else at a white elephant party. Web users go elsewhere, and you are left to figure out where they went and what they wanted.

If you do not take the time to understand your users, you can expect they will abandon your site and go to your competitors'. As a result, a good portion of your website maintenance will go to correcting your lack of user understanding.

Not understanding your users will also cost you a lot of money in lost opportunity. **Figure 8.13** shows bounce rates, average time on site, and percentage of new visitors from a website that management thought was running great because they assumed they knew their users. That was until they put web analytics on the site.

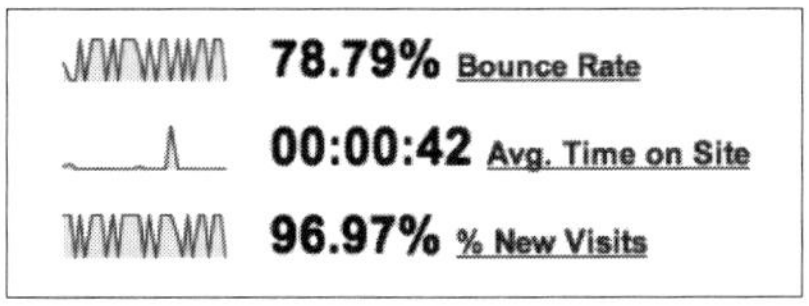

⋀⋀⋁⋀⋁⋀⋀	**78.79%**	Bounce Rate
___⋀__	**00:00:42**	Avg. Time on Site
⋀⋀⋁⋁⋀⋀⋀	**96.97%**	% New Visits

FIGURE 8.13 Only 3 percent to 4 percent of users return to this site.

The results in Figure 8.13 show a bounce rate of almost 80 percent. This means that almost four out of five users who hit the website immediately leave. Of the 20 percent who stay, they are staying for less than 45 seconds. The percentage of new visits (almost 97 percent) tells us the vast majority of users are new visitors. Only 3 percent to 4 percent of users returned to the site.

To sum it up, almost 100 percent of this site's visitors are leaving in under 42 seconds and are never coming back. This is an example of a website that was built under the assumptions that management could build a site without any feedback from users.

Know your users before you build

The more you know about your users the better your site will be. What you want to know before you build is

- What type of **information** are your users looking for? (How to satisfy an informational search)
- What do they expect to **do** on your site? (How to satisfy a transactional search)
- What **motivates** users to use your website? (How to engender trust and emotions)

You have more freedom to make changes in the beginning of the design process than later in the process. Find out as much as you can about your users in the beginning so you can apply as much as you can into the design before the code is written and design freedom is lost or severely limited.

Try to get as much information as possible from users in the beginning of the project. Use interviews, observations, focus groups, surveys, and combinations of these data-gathering methods. It will save you hours, money, and headaches later.

What do your users expect?

There is no way to account for all the types of behaviors users will display on the search engines or on your website. Search usability is an iterative process. Just like your website, search usability is never 100 percent complete. There is always something to test. Something to improve. Something to measure.

CASE STUDY
INTERNATIONAL TRAVEL SITE

Websites that "use the users' language" often generate a higher return on investment than sites that don't. There are a variety of ways that website owners can determine the "users' language," including many keyword research tools that the web search engines provide. Search engine optimization (SEO) pros use these tools all the time to determine how web searchers find their client's official site and their client's competitors' sites.

Without direct, one-on-one contact with actual site visitors, keyword research tools can lead business owners and SEO professionals down the wrong path. Here is an example.

During usability testing on an international travel site, we tested the site's information architecture (categorization and labels) in multiple languages: American English, British English, French, and Spanish. In particular, we were determining how the keyword phrase *student housing* was used in different cultures.

Online keyword research data showed the word for *student* (in French, *étudiant* or *étudiants*) as a good navigation label because students typically have different income levels and needs than other groups of people. The keyword research data showed that many French-language searchers used the word *étudiant* or *étudiants* to find accommodations for student travelers on a limited budget. Therefore, our client wanted the word *étudiant* implemented in several different navigation labels.

Usability testing generated some interesting responses. Almost every time the French phrase for *student housing* appeared on a web page, test participants noticeably paused and looked confused. When we asked why they hesitated, they said that the phrase was not appropriate for a travel website. To them, *student housing* or *student accommodations* meant dormitories, where students can live while attending college.

The French participants then placed the student-related information groupings in one of two piles:

- **Discard.** Participants felt that the information label and/or grouping did not belong on the website at all.
- **Do not know.** Participants were unsure whether the information label and/or grouping belonged on the website.

Over 90 percent of French test participants placed student-related information in the discard pile. In fact, usability tests in the other three languages had nearly the same outcome.

Even though keyword research tools are one means of discovering the users' language, they should not be the only way to determine the text on navigation labels and other information scents.

SEO professionals often apply keyword research data to a website and end up creating a site architecture that is confusing to both search engines and site visitors. It is hard to make correct inferences without watching users attempting to complete a task you've given them. Usability testing combined with keyword research data provides the most accurate navigation solutions.

It is very difficult to design a simple site the first time out of the gate that meets or exceeds the goals of users and the business.

Why you might not get your website right the first time:

- There are no perfect user interfaces.
- There are no perfect information architectures.
- There are no perfect designs.
- There is no average user.

There are, however

- Smart user interfaces
- Smart information architectures
- Smart designs

How to be smart:

- Get feedback from users early in the process, even before design.
- Apply your findings in your initial design.
- Test your design with a candidate user and sample tasks and get feedback.
- Repeat.

NOTE Testing one user can make the site better for everyone.

How management's decisions affect web usability

We once worked with a company whose flagship product was Internet fax. Internet fax is a service that allows you to send and receive faxes over the Internet through your email just like you would send an email. No fax machine is needed. It's a very convenient service.

Unfortunately, the company was losing money quarter after quarter. They decided to be in the document management business despite the fact that the majority of revenue was generated by Internet faxing. Document management comes in many flavors. For the sake of this story, know that Internet faxing is not the same as the document management.

Part of the initiative to be in the document management business was to position the website to speak to investors. The company made investors the primary target audience of the website with no regard for customers or prospects.

Management decided that they would no longer refer to their faxing services as *fax*. Instead, they renamed their fax service to a very arbitrary name. The name they chose didn't mention fax or have any connection to fax whatsoever.

The website soon fell out of natural search results. Users who had formerly located the site via navigational searches due to referrals were confused because they couldn't find the fax services they heard about from their colleagues and friends. These users abandoned the site.

Users who located the website by means other than search engines were not able to find the fax service they were looking for. They weren't able to orient themselves on the home page because they never found the word *fax* anywhere on the page. These users abandoned as well.

The users who didn't immediately bounce off the home page tried using the site search. Zero results for *fax* were found. Other users tried pogo-sticking around the site, unable to find what they were looking for. They abandoned too.

Management broke the big rule of using the users' language in hopes of being something they were not to investors. And as a result, management alienated their prospects and achieved the self-fulfilling prophecy that the company could not be sustained on Internet fax revenue alone. The company was sold a few years later.

Market Researchers and Search Usability

Usability testing is misunderstood. If you tell a market researcher you are interested in usability testing, they will probably come back with something like:

"Great, I'll set up a focus group right away!" or "Great, I'll send out a survey right away!"

So, what is the difference between usability tests and focus groups?

Focus groups, surveys, and other research methods are very valuable, but they are not usability tests. Market research will not tell you why users do the following:

- Browse on your website
- Pogo-stick on your website (**Figure 8.14**)
- Forage on your website
- Scan or read your website's content
- Use your website's search functionality (site search)
- Orient on your website
- Perform a query on a commercial search engine
- Click the back button
- If they use site search
- If they use your site map

Only with usability tests will you get a full picture of **how** and **why** users search on the commercial search engines and on your website.

FIGURE 8.14 Site visitors often exhibit pogo-sticking behavior but do not realize that they do it.

Why focus groups aren't usability tests

Focus group participants may tell you that they want specific information and functionality on your website, but you really do not know if that's true until you usability test.

In one study, participants taking part in a focus group on how consumers might evaluate health information on the web suggested that they wanted to know

- The source of the health information published on the website

- If the information came from an individual or an institution

- If the information was based on science or an individual's experience

Corresponding usability tests told a story contrary to the statements made in the focus groups. Researchers found

- Participants did not actively search for who stood behind the sites.

- Participants did not actively search for how the information had been compiled.

The conclusion: People say one thing, but do another. Therefore, do usability testing if you want to know how users will use your site.

Why surveys aren't usability tests

Imagine asking your customers the following survey questions:

1. When searching on Company A's website, I tend to pogo-stick:
   - Strongly Disagree
   - Disagree
   - Neutral
   - Agree
   - Strongly Agree

2. I lose the scent of information on Company A's website:
   - Never
   - Almost Never
   - Sometimes
   - Frequently
   - Always

3. Rate Company A's site on its ability to help you orient yourself:
   - Poor
   - Below Average
   - Average
   - Above Average
   - Outstanding

4. When on Google I primarily perform:
   - Navigational queries
   - Informational queries
   - Transactional queries

Trying to get information from users about their search behavior just isn't possible without usability testing. If you want to know how users search on the web, you need to watch them use the web.

IT and Search Usability

An IT group could be referred to by many different titles depending on your organization. You may know them as programmers, developers, software engineers, or information technology (IT). They are a very valuable resource that is often asked to stretch beyond their skill set in ways that frequently wreak havoc with users.

Building websites using iterative design

The iterative design model was developed in response to unhappy users and exceeds budgets of traditional design. Using the iterative design model, you observe users using the website in many states of development, including rough paper prototypes, graphic mockups, and functioning interfaces. The iterative design model refines the website building process by getting constant feedback from users through multiple rounds of prototyping, user testing, and analysis.

Developers found the most successful websites get feedback from users from the beginning of the project. They also found that websites built using the iterative design model were more likely to go live on time and within budget.

Even with the success of iterative design, many developers prefer to build websites the traditional way, delaying search usability efforts until the project is live. The old model of throwing requirements over the wall to IT and getting a finished product back in three months doesn't work. It never really did. By iteratively testing your search usability efforts before going live, you can make improvements, thereby achieving greater results for your client or employer and delivering a better user experience to your users. Design must be iterative if search usability is to succeed.

Losing the scent of information

The scent of information can be lost in many ways. In the world of developers, it happens through user errors, URL structure, and site search.

Losing the scent—error messages

What's the use of driving traffic to a website only to have users abandon halfway through the checkout process because of an insufficient error message?

Poorly written error messages results in frustrated users and the loss of the scent of information. If users cannot figure out what happened because of an incoherent error message, they abandon. Programmers are typically the ones who end up writing the error messages. They do so as an afterthought when working in the code. So what happens when users encounter a poor error message?

NOTE When writing error messages, write in English, French, Japanese, or whatever language your users speak. Whatever you do, do not write in tech-ese.

If you're really lucky, your users will incorrectly blame themselves for triggering an error message, feel dumb and pick up the phone, use click to chat, or click to call to have a real person help them.

If you're really, really lucky, your users will incorrectly blame themselves for triggering an error, feel dumb, muddle through the error message, figure out what went wrong, and proceed through the checkout.

However, if your site is like most websites, you will not be so lucky, and users will abandon at an alarming rate.

Losing the scent—URL structure

IT isn't concerned with URL structure as long as the URL serves up a web page. This is true for almost everything that IT touches in terms of web usability. As long as it works technically, IT is moving on to a new project. It doesn't matter that users cannot use it.

URL structure communicates to users the organization of your web site. Some sites do this better than others.

Let's take a look at www.marthastewart.com, specifically the URL for Martha's Valentine's Day recipes. You can tell by looking at the URL that the page is about Valentine's Day recipes but it takes a while.

Actual URL: http://www.marthastewart.com/valentines-day-holiday-recipes?lnc=f804758a65cee010VgnVCM1000003d370a0aRCRD&rsc=leftnav_holiday_valentines-day

A cleaner URL with less code gibberish would communicate important information much quicker.

Proposed URL: http://www.marthastewart.com/holidays/valentines-day/valentines-day-holiday-recipes

This proposed URL communicates the information architecture and gives users a sense of what they might find on the site.

To savvy users, the proposed URL communicates that in order to get to "Valentine's Day recipes" you have to click through "holidays" and then "Valentine's Day."

The proposed URL communicates that the site might offer information on holidays other than just Valentine's Day, because "holidays" is part of the URL string. The URL also communicates that there might be more information on Valentine's Day than just recipes because "valentines-day-holiday-recipes" is a subdirectory of "valentines-day."

From a SERP point of view, a more descriptive URL is more intuitive for users who are trying to choose from the SERP listings. Compare the URLs in Martha Stewart's Valentine's Day recipe page to Hershey's. The Hershey's URL is more descriptive and contains keywords that give a good scent of information. The Martha Stewart URL contains similar keywords, but also contains a string that detracts from the scent of information by adding unnecessary noise.

FIGURES 8.15 Martha Stewart's complex URL.

Valentine's Day recipes and more holiday recipes, crafts projects ...
Valentine's Day recipes. Goat-Cheese "Ravioli" · Personalized Chocolates · Hot Chocolate ... 2008 Martha Stewart Living Omnimedia, Inc. All rights reserved. ...
www.marthastewart.com/ valentines-day-holiday-recipes?
lnc=f804758a65cee010VgnVCM1000003d370a0aRCRD&rsc... - 54k - Cached - Similar pages

FIGURES 8.16 Hershey's descriptive URL.

HERSHEY'S Valentine's Day – Valentine's Day Recipes
Sweeten up the mood with a Valentine's Day recipe from HERSHEY'S. There are Valentine's Day recipes for cookies, cakes, and other treats. ...
www.hersheys.com/valentines/recipes/ - 14k - Cached - Similar pages

Losing the scent—site searches

Using site search doesn't have to mean losing the scent of information, but it commonly does. According to Jared Spool, once users turn to site search their failure rate rises to about 70 percent as opposed to 47 percent without using site search.

So who owns this 70 percent abandon rate? The responsibility of site search usually falls under IT, not because it's an IT job, but because IT or someone else thinks it's an IT job. In reality, the primary owners of site search should be information architects as they are the ones responsible for the organization of information.

You should consider a few things when creating your site search. First, consider if you should provide site search at all. If you cannot implement site search well, you might want to consider skipping it.

If you decide to use it, consider the following:

- **Most importantly, try to limit the use of site search.** Work with an information architect on the labels used in primary and secondary navigation and a usability professional on contextual and related links. The more obvious your navigational elements are, the less your users will use site search and other supplemental navigation.

- **Watch users use your site.** At what point do they use site search? That's the point where they have lost the scent of information. Try to correct the problem to reduce site search use. Research has shown that following links (instead of searching) exposes users to more pages they can use. Also, task success goes up (assuming the link structure creates a clear scent leading to the goal). On the other hand, some tasks benefit from search: finding a book using a title or author; or finding a phone number and address using a person's name, and so on. These would be called "exact searches." Computers serve these goals well.

- **Work collectively**. Get IT and information architects to work collaboratively on site search to determine what results show, the formatting of those results, and the keywords used in the site search results.

- **Observe user interaction with search results**. Similar to their use of commercial search engines, most users do not go beyond the first page of the search results. Test how users respond to more than the typical 10 results per page. Change the number of search results to 20, 30, or 40 results per page.

- **Find out what your users are searching for**. Mine the data from your site search to make your website and site search better. Consider incorporating the language used in site search into your website's information architecture as labels and in tips, FAQs, and other content pages of your website. Make sure these new pages show in your site search as well.

NOTE For more information and resources to help you build site search, see *Information Architecture for the World Wide Web*, Third Edition by Peter Morville and Louis Rosenfield (O'Reilly Publishing, 2006).

- **Anticipate user intent.** Many queries entered in site search are going to be informational searches. What other types of information can you present that is relevant to their query?

When done well, site search can reduce site abandonment and get users back on track.

Avoiding unnecessary features

As a rule of thumb, the more features something has the more difficult it is to find those features and the more difficult it is to use those features.

So what's the problem, you ask? Developers love features. They love to put features on websites that users have no interest in.

At what point do more features become unnecessary? Before adding more features to a website, ask yourself a few questions:

- What is the benefit to the users?
- Do the users value the benefit?
- Did the users express interest in the feature?
- Will the user value the feature on your website?

Features are only cool if users think they're cool. Users may find features annoying and distracting. Avoid worshipping the cool. Focus on the useful and relevant.

Information Architects and Search Usability

Information architects organize the web pages to make content easier to find. Their work is the foundation of any website and search usability.

Information architects are not graphic artists or programmers. They aren't terribly concerned with how a website looks. They do care about how a website functions, however they do not code the functionality.

Information architects' work includes

- Defining navigational elements and labels
- Organizing sequence and content of web pages
- Determining breadth and depth of a website navigation scheme
- Defining the appropriate titles for pages
- Developing an optimal framework that supports findability and search usability
- Developing wireframes (blueprints of web pages) in PowerPoint or other tools

Depending on the individual and organization, information architects might also cover

- Task analysis
- Interaction design
- Real-time responsiveness goals
- Usability evaluation, usability testing
- Assessing conformance to usability standards

Information architects simplify complexity, determine navigational controls, and understand what information is needed for users to accomplish tasks and find information. Information architects are responsible for

- Reducing the number of clicks needed to complete a task or to find information
- Reduce the number of windows needed to complete a task or to find information
- Reduce the learning curve of websites so users can complete tasks and find information more efficiently

NOTE If you find yourself going straight to the computer to design, you're probably skipping a few very important steps in the web design process. You could not turn a computer on for days and still be designing a website. You can do all of your upfront work such as research, information architecture, and wireframing without a computer. You only really need a computer when you get into graphic design and coding.

It's all uphill without good information architecture

One of the biggest and most common mistakes made when building websites is when graphic designers go straight to Adobe Photoshop or a similar graphics program and start designing. This is like a construction company starting to construct a building without a blueprint.

Do you think someone hands a construction company a truckload of bricks and tells them to start building? Of course not. Then why do web designers begin building with no information architecture or wireframes to guide their decision-making? They shouldn't, but it happens.

Bad information architecture will cripple your search usability efforts.

The danger of going right into Adobe Photoshop at the beginning of the design process is that a good-looking design can cover up inferior information architecture. Bad information architecture will cripple your search usability efforts.

In addition to covering up bad information architecture, heading straight into graphic design at the beginning of the process frequently takes the attention away from the information architecture as the team becomes consumed with conversations about colors, fonts, and photos.

Look and feel, and the emotions evoked from images, are very important, but those shouldn't be pursued at the expense of the website information architecture. More thought and discussion is typically put into a photograph that can be easily swapped out than the backbone of the site—the information architecture. This needs to change if search usability is to succeed.

ARE TWO PAGES BETTER THAN ONE?
A SHORT STORY ABOUT INFORMATION ARCHITECTURE

A colleague of ours told us this story. He was hired as an SEO consultant but knew a thing or two about information architecture. He noticed some architectural inconsistencies and spamming concerns on the site and brought them up to the marketing manager responsible for managing the website.

SEO consultant: "Did you know you have two of the exact same pages on your site?"

Client: "No, we do not."

SEO consultant: "Yes, you do." (Emails the client the two URLs)

Client: "Oh, right. I think it's OK."

SEO consultant: "The pages are being used incorrectly. The higher level category page should be a landing page that serves as the table of contents for this section. It should be used as a pathway to get users to their desired content."

Client: "Uh-huh."

SEO consultant: "The other page is one of five content pages that houses the actual information under the section. It's a parent-child relationship. It's what people expect from a website and is how your other sections are set up. The way it's currently set up will be confusing to the users."

Client: "Users will figure it out."

SEO consultant: "Users will figure it out? Have you ever read a book that had the same page published twice?"

Client: "No. Why would you print the same page twice in book?"

SEO consultant: "You wouldn't. You shouldn't print the same page twice on a website either."

Client: (Long pause) "We'll change the page."

If you want to get users to the information they want, you need to set up your information architecture to make that happen. Our colleague's experience illustrates how having your feet in multiple disciplines can help your client build a better website.

Information architecture versus quality assurance

In many organizations, more time is spent on quality assurance (QA) than preparing a website for good information architecture. If your information architecture and your wireframes are not thoroughly thought out, you will be wasting your time proofing a site that isn't worth proofing to begin with.

This misbalance between IA and QA is partially due to

- The lack of understanding what an information architect is
- The lack of understanding how an information architect's work affects website design and search usability
- An unqualified need to see a tangible graphic design by management
- Unrealistic timelines that result in projects that exceed budgets and compromise quality

Top-loading your process with surveys, interviews, thesaurus research, web logs, usability tests, and keyword research will culminate in a solid information architecture that will act as your foundation for search usability.

■ CONCLUSION

Key points of this chapter:

- Search usability is everyone's job. Many times there are no clear lines to define when an SEO professional's job begins and ends and when a graphic designer, copywriter, or information architect's job begins and ends.
- It's all about perspective. The more you understand other web professional disciplines the better you can manage, implement, and measure search usability.
- Not every page element can be the most important thing on the web page. Page elements must be created with a visual hierarchy. If not, everything will appear to be equally visually weighted and search usability will suffer. Use design principles to consciously evoke a "top down" flow or hierarchy.
- By using the users' language in critical areas of web pages and formatting copy appropriately, writers can keep feeding users the scent of information.
- A poor search usability experience equals a poor brand experience. Improve your users' brand experience online by reducing their use of the back button and pogo-sticking.

- If you are going to use supplemental navigation like site maps and site search, put the enough resources behind them to make them work for your users.

- Crises happen. Plan to manage your brand online by considering how users will look for information in times of crisis.

- Usability professionals need to stop ignoring querying behavior. They must also include keyword research when they talk about using the users' language.

- You can expect your users who find your site in search engines to be more targeted and better-quality traffic than other sources of online traffic.

- Instead of assuming you know what users want from your site, ask them. The more you know about your users in the beginning of the process, the less reworking you will need to do later.

- Focus groups aren't usability tests. Surveys aren't usability tests. Usability tests are usability tests. Ask people who could be your site users to show you how to complete a given task. Ask them to "think out loud." Make notes of their experiences. Tell them "we are not testing you, we are testing the design." Take notes on problems.

- Interactive development, showing your site to potential users at each stage, leads to successful search usability.

- Losing the scent of information can happen in many ways. In the world of developers it results from user errors, URL structure, and site search.

- More features mean more usability problems for users. More features also mean reduced success in finding what users are truly looking for.

- Search usability begins with good information architecture.

CHAPTER 9

HOW TO IMPROVE YOUR WEBSITE'S SEARCH USABILITY

This chapter gives you web usability tests you can conduct to improve your website's search usability and increase conversions. It also addresses myths and misconceptions about search and web usability.

You don't need to go through a rigorous recruiting process to find participants to run the usability tests described in this chapter. If you have research personnel and budget that you can leverage to get feedback from users, great. If you find yourself in an "if you want something done right, you have to do it yourself" scenario, try talking with a friend, neighbor, or colleague to get a different perspective on your website.

The idea is to get valuable, actionable feedback to continually improve your website's search and web usability. Let's take a look at a few usability tests and other techniques that will help.

■ IDEAL TEST PARTICIPANTS

Before you can conduct any usability test, you'll need test participants. You want to find people who are representative users of your website. For example, if you're trying to sell tennis shoes on your site, test people who wear tennis shoes. If you are testing a travel website, choose participants who book flights and/or car rentals online.

Some websites might be more difficult to recruit for than others. If you can't find ideal test candidates, ask the next-best candidates to "role play" your users. Give them some background or create a story to help them identify with the part. The more detailed you can make your story, the better your participants will be able to play the role.

If you test participants that you feel are less-than-ideal candidates, consider the qualities that make them not ideal and factor those qualities into your assessments of your test findings. Not being able to find the ideal test participants shouldn't prevent you from testing your site.

Generally speaking, there are a few things that make some test candidates better than others, whether they are your ideal test participants or not.

Qualities you want in a test participant

- Someone who is comfortable thinking out loud.

- Someone who isn't familiar with your site, assuming you need to test for first-time user interaction.

- Someone who is familiar with your site, assuming you want to improve your website for repeat visitors.

- Someone who will be able to understand the language.

Qualities you want to avoid in a test participant

- Someone who is trying to please you and doesn't want to hurt your feelings.

- Someone who doesn't use the web (email use is not the same as web use). You are not designing for the newbie who is just getting familiar with scroll bars and radio buttons.

- Someone who finds your site easy because he or she has extensive domain knowledge—more than most users do. His or her performance on your site might overshadow issues for less-knowledgeable users.

- Someone who doesn't have the minimal amount of domain knowledge that you need your user to have. This user will be stumped at every turn on your website.

Additionally, you'll also want to avoid web developers and web designers in your test group. Developers will probably view your site as a challenge and try to figure it out, and web designers will tend to tell you how to redesign your site rather than showing you how they would actually use it.

Be sure to communicate to your test participants that it's the website that is being tested, not them. They will still feel like they are the ones being tested. Inevitably, you will get at least one user per test group who asks, "How'd I do?" Tell them they gave great feedback, and thank them for their time.

Additionally, tell the participants not to worry about hurting your feelings. Tell them that testing is a way to learn how people interact with the website so that you can improve it for everyone who uses it. You can expect to pay up to $100 an hour for your participants' time. This might seem like a lot to some people, but it's pennies compared to the time it takes when your test participants don't show, and you need to start your recruiting from scratch all over again. If you are testing with co-workers, offer to buy them lunch or give them movie tickets. If you are a small business owner in need of participants, offer dinner to family members and friends in exchange for being a test participant.

■ REVERSE CARD SORT TEST

The reverse card sort test will help you fit new content into an existing website in a way that makes your products and services easy to find for search engines and for users. This test will also help you assess whether adding new content is a natural fit for your existing website, or if the content is a patch for a compromised information architecture.

Most usability tests need about five to 10 participants per group to generate meaningful results. Some research suggests that you need upwards of 15 users for a reverse card sort test. Generally speaking, you know you have tested with enough users when you stop hearing feedback unique to each participant and start hearing consistent, similar feedback from your test group. For reverse card sorting, you are looking for trends in how users organize the information. An 80 percent or better accuracy rate is a reasonable goal for reverse card sorting.

Before we get to how to apply the reverse card sort test to an existing website, let's first take a look how to conduct the test using cards. You can use index cards or pre-formatted labels for your reverse card sort testing. Use what you have handy and/or feel most comfortable using. If you hand-write the labels on the cards, make sure your writing is legible.

In **Figure 9.1**, notice the predefined categories at the top that include colors, flowers, and fruit. We've also included a few blank cards in case participants come up with a new (and possibly better) category or category label. Also, notice the nine large cards below the category cards that include *red, peach, green,* and so on.

Under which category would you expect to find each of the nine cards? Would you prefer to create your own category labels?

FIGURE 9.1 The layout of a reverse card sort test before a test participant categorizes the cards. Note the predefined categories and blank cards at the top and the predefined cards with labels grouped below.

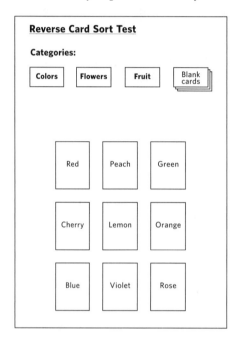

Figure 9.2 shows two possible results of the reverse card sort test. One test participant classified *orange* as a fruit and another test participant classified *orange* as a color. When there is more than one category that a test participant identifies a card with, they might look to you to confirm their choice or might tell you that they would put the card under more than one category. You might have had the same thoughts as you were trying to organize the cards in Figure 9.1. As the conductor of the test, you should encourage test participants to choose a category and remind them there is no wrong answer. You want them to commit to a category so you understand how they would group the information.

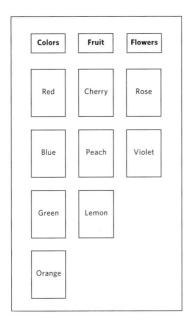 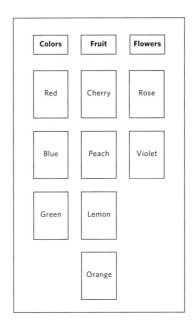

FIGURE 9.2 *Orange* was classified as a color by one test participant and as a fruit by another.

Figure 9.3 is another example of how a test participant categorized the cards. In this case, the test participant thought that *cherry* referred to cherry blossom, *peach* referred to peach blossom, and *lemon* referred to lemon blossom. They saw no need to use the *fruit* category.

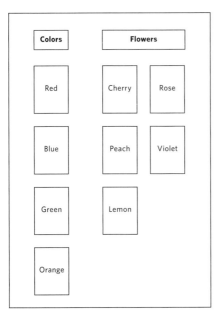

FIGURE 9.3 Some participants didn't even use the *fruit* category.

Let's apply the reverse card sort test to the National Cancer Institute website in **Figure 9.4**. In lieu of colors, flowers, and fruit, use the top-level navigation tabs as main categories of the website.

FIGURE 9.4 In a reverse card sort usability test, you do not have to show the entire web page. You can, as in this example, only show participants the main categories.

Looking at the National Cancer Institute primary navigation in Figure 9.4, where you would expect to find the following information:

1. Latest information about breast cancer treatment
2. Cancer information for physicians and other healthcare professionals
3. Calendar of events
4. Most common types of cancer
5. Risk factors for pancreatic cancer

You generally encounter one of three scenarios while conducting the reverse card sort test:

- **Scenario 1:** Everyone places the content under the same primary navigation link. This scenario is ideal and is also the most unlikely. Few websites are this cut and dried.

- **Scenario 2:** The majority of your users place the content under one primary navigation link while the others place the content under other primary navigation links. This is the most likely situation.

- **Scenario 3:** No matter how many users you test, you don't see any trends in how your users organize the content. This occurs with sites that have poorly labeled primary navigation buttons.

You have nothing to worry about if most of the responses fall into Scenario 1, when there is consensus among your test participants as to where they would look for content. Simply add the content under the category your test participants chose.

In Scenario 2, the majority (as note earlier, an 80 percent accuracy or better is a reasonable goal) of your users are telling you where they expect to find the content. Listen to the majority and place your content where they believe it belongs.

You'll need to perform an additional step for the remaining users who looked for your new content under the other primary navigation links. Ask these users on which page under the primary navigation links they selected would they expect to find the content. These users are telling you which pages should include a cross-reference link to the new content to get them back on the scent. For best results, annotate the cross-reference with keywords to increase the scent of information.

If you find yourself in a Scenario 3 situation, chances are you need to reexamine your site's information architecture as the reverse card sorting isn't yielding meaningful results.

The reverse card sort test can also help organize content at a secondary level. Imagine you want to apply keyword and corresponding content to existing Frequently Asked Questions (FAQs) pages. Imagine you have a preexisting list of FAQs organized under five categories. You want to add additional FAQs to your pages but you aren't sure how to organize them. Using the reverse card sort test, show your users the five FAQ categories and ask them under which FAQ category they would expect to locate the new questions.

Many search engine optimization (SEO) professionals find themselves working with clients who do not want to change their website architecture but still want to implement SEO by adding new optimized content. The reverse card sort will help organize new content if your website architecture already makes sense to your users. If the website structure doesn't make sense to your users, consider reengineering the architecture as users will have a difficult time finding information on your site and adding new content will just add to the noise.

NOTE A card sort test allows website users to group site content in a way that makes sense to them. The idea is that if your website is organized in a way that makes sense to your users, they will have an easier time locating information on your site. For more information on card sorting go to http://www.usability.gov/design/cardsort.html or http://en.wikipedia.org/wiki/Card_sorting.

■ ONE-ON-ONE FIELD INTERVIEWS

Use one-on-one interviews to ask users what type of information they want from your website, and what they want to do when they get to your website. By understanding the type of information and functionality your users expect from your site, you can begin to build a customized keyword list that will help users find your site on the commercial search engines for information and transactional queries.

One-on-one interviews give you the potential to build a keyword list that is unique to your audience and your website. One-on-one interviews also give you the opportunity to ask follow-up questions. You can clear up any misunderstandings and find out more about your users' needs and interests, potentially generating more content for other page types such as FAQs and how-to pages.

During the interview, make a list of the keywords users say out loud when they express themselves. Note how they talk about performing a task and the type of information they would like to find on your website.

TIP One-on-one interviews aren't meant to be a substitute for online keyword research tools. Use one-on-one interviews in conjunction with online keyword research tools to create a unique list of keywords to optimize your website.

After the interview, compare your user feedback with the information and functionality your site currently features and the priorities attributed to your content and functionality when you first built your site. Is your site matching up to users' expectations or is there a disconnect between what your users expect and what your website offers?

One-on-one user interviews can very well be the beginning of creating new categories, subcategories, FAQs, tips, and other content-rich pages and functionalities for your website.

You can walk away from one-on-one interviews with a competitive edge if you listen to the subtle and sometimes not-so-subtle differences in how your users express what they want to find and what they want to do on your site.

■ FUNCTIONAL SALIENCE TEST

Note The functional salience test was adapted from Eric Schaffer's *Institutionalization of Usability: A Step-by-Step Guide*. Find more of Eric Schaffer's usability tests at https://www.informit.com/articles/article.aspx?p=170791&seqNum=5

Functional salience tests help usability professionals determine and prioritize the functionality of software applications. The functional salience test was born of the necessity to limit the number of options available in a software application. Users frequently say yes when offered functionality, resulting in an application that has too many functions and controls to make it useful.

You can use a variation of the functional salience test to determine the most relevant page interlinks available to site visitors from any one page, including contextual links, upsell links, and alternative links. This test should exclude global and local navigational items, as those navigational elements should be constant across the site and/or categories where appropriate.

Begin the test by describing the page in question to a user. For the purpose of this example, let's use a product page that features running shoes. You could verbally describe the page as featuring a pair of running shoes for the more serious runner who typically runs three or more miles a day, totaling 20-plus miles a week. Many of the runners who use these running shoes run in 5K and 10K races, and half and full marathons.

Ideally test participants should be representative of an audience who would find your page useful. Don't ask someone who has little or no interest or knowledge in the page topic or product, as you'll get skewed data. After you describe your page, give your participants a list of interlinks they might have available to them. Tell them that they can choose only three of those options from the page in question. In the case of a product page that sells running shoes, the options you would offer to test participants might look like this:

- Similar running shoes
- Running jackets
- Running shorts
- Running socks
- Running pants
- Running training tips
- How to train for your first marathon
- Find a race near you

Just like software users, chances are your website users will want more information than is good for them and will want to design a site that has everything at their fingertips, resulting in a website that is overcrowded and full of noise—dramatically decreasing the ability of site visitors to search and find information.

By forcing test participants to select the information that is most important to them, we can limit the number of links to the most important ones. As a result, we will be creating a site that meets users' mental models and a site with content that is more easily found.

■ HOME PAGE EXPECTANCY TEST

Use this test to make sure you are properly communicating content that is accessible from the home page. Document the content the user expects as well as the media type and formatting such as a PDF or a video. The closer you can match your content and execution to your users' expectations, the better the experience will be for them. The home page expectancy test will need to be done in two steps:

1. **Click affordance.** Print out your home page and give it to test participants. Ask them to circle everything they believe to be a hyperlink on the page.

2. **Expected content.** Ask the participants what information they would expect to find or what they would expect to do if they were to click one of the links they circled.

> **TIP** It's best to conduct a preliminary test with a co-worker to get the kinks out of your test before testing with participant(s). Any co-worker will do. What you are doing is testing your test to make sure you haven't missed anything in your preparation. This will ensure a smoother execution of the test with your participants.

Step 1: Click Affordance Test

NOTE Don Norman was the first to apply the term *affordance* to user experience in *The Design of Everyday Things*.

Affordance is the visual indication of how an object functions—in other words, what it is for. In an ideal world you would be able to perceive an object's affordance without having to handle the object but simply by looking at it.

For example, there is no need to pick up a pencil to know that it *affords* writing, or a hat to know that it *affords* wearing on your head. If you have to ask yourself, "What is this for" or "What does this do," the affordance of the object is not clear and will require more cognitive processing to determine its function.

One way affordance applies in the hypertext medium of the World Wide Web is through the perceived clickability of web page elements. Page elements that are clickable should look clickable. It's just as important that items that are not clickable don't look clickable as we don't want users randomly clicking around the page, getting frustrated, getting angry, and eventually abandoning.

The importance of click affordance was illustrated by one of our participants being tested on a website that didn't underline links. She said angrily, "Why don't websites underline links any more? I don't understand why they change something just to change it without making it better." She said this just before she abandoned the assigned task.

Test for click affordance with paper prototypes, more advanced graphical prototypes, or even a page screen shot. Whatever you do, don't test with a functioning website. Affordance tests aren't to determine if a user notices if the arrow turns into a hand when the user moves the mouse pointer over something that is clickable, but that's exactly what you'll be testing if you use a functioning website. Test to see what users perceive to be clickable elements on the web page. The only way to do this is to get users away from the computer so they aren't tempted to rollover page elements to see if the arrow changes. In their natural environment, users determine if something is clickable or not *before* they move the mouse, not when they rollover something. Again, it's the perception of what is clickable that you are testing.

Begin the click affordance test by giving the test participants the paper prototype, graphic prototype, or hardcopy screen shot. Ask them to circle everything on the page they think is clickable. Chances are, your participants won't circle every actual link. They might even circle some page elements that are not links. Some participants will circle big blocks of content; others will be very specific and will circle only one or two words. You might have to gently ask some of them to clarify what they think is a link and what isn't a link.

Don't lead your participants by acting surprised when they don't circle something you think is obviously a hyperlink. Also, don't ask "Don't you think the big graphic on the right is a link?" or other types of questions that will taint your results.

Looking at the National Cancer Institute page (**Figure 9.5**), what would you think is clickable?

FIGURE 9.5 A content page from the National Cancer Institute's website did well in a click affordance test. www.cancer.gov/newscenter/pressreleases/ALTTO

The National Cancer Institute website did well in an affordance test, but did experience the problems shown in **Table 9.1**.

TABLE 9.1 National Cancer Institute's click affordance test results

POTENTIAL PROBLEM AREAS	LINK OR NO LINK
"En español" in the left column	Link, but the users didn't think so
The icons to the left of the print and email links	Link, but the users didn't think so
Images above **Posted**: 02/29/2008	Not a link, but the users thought so

If users miss a hyperlink, they miss it. Note it silently to yourself or have an observer write it down, and move on.

Let's take a look at **Figure 9.6** on the next page to see how Google communicates clickability.

TIP Anything your participants don't circle that is a hyperlink should be noted. Make changes to these elements to make them look more clickable. If hyperlinked elements don't look clickable, they fail the affordance test.

National **Cancer Institute** - Comprehensive **Cancer** Information
Accurate, up-to-date, comprehensive **cancer** information from the US government's principal agency for **cancer** research.
www.**cancer**.gov/ - 35k - Cached - Similar pages

A to Z List of Cancers	Prostate Cancer
Breast Cancer	Cancers by Body Location/System
Clinical Trials	Partnering On Education Tools ...
Lung Cancer	Colon

Step 2: Expected Content Test

After your users return your paper prototype, graphic prototype, or hardcopy screen shot, ask them what they would expect to find or be able to do after clicking each of the "links" they circled.

What users tell you they expect to find after clicking is what they will be scanning for on the page that follows their click. If users don't find what they are looking for on that page, they will lose the scent of information.

Users may also circle items that are not links. You'll want to know what page elements your participants thought were links and what they expected from clicking those page elements. This may be an opportunity to make a page element a hyperlink or you may need to rethink the visual treatment of the page element as it is incorrectly communicating clickablity.

Some items to keep in mind as you administer the test:

- Did your participants expect to begin transacting with your site by clicking any of the links? Did they think they were going to download a whitepaper, play a game, or submit a form?

- Did your participants expect information that isn't currently on the site? Would they be disappointed if they were to click the actual link and find information other that what they anticipated would be there?

- What type of technology did your participants expect to deliver the information or transaction? Did they expect a pop-up, a new page, a new website, a PDF, a Flash application, or Ajax application?

The closer you can match your web links to the expectations of your participants the better the chance you have of meeting your website goals and not losing users.

■ EIGHT-SECOND USABILITY TEST ON CONTENT PAGES

The eight-second usability test is adapted from Jared Spool's five-second usability test with three notable differences:

- Jared's test takes five seconds; ours takes eight.
- The second difference is where the testing begins. Jared begins on the content page, starting his five-second count when the user first sees the page. We begin our test in the SERP, and start the eight-second count after the user clicks the SERP listing and the viewable portion of the content page is loaded. We'll explain this in detail in a minute.
- The third and final difference is the goals of the tests. Jared's test is designed to understand users' initial impression of a content page. Our test is designed to do that too, but also to understand if they feel like they are on the right page after they click the SERP listing, if the information they want is on the resulting page, and if they can establish a sense of place on this page. We give the user three more seconds to allow for download time as well as the time it takes to cognitively process and determine a sense of place and note keywords on the resulting page.

NOTE You can find out more about Jared's five-second test at www.uie.com/articles/five_second_test/

It's very important that you don't tell users you are only going to give them eight seconds to look at the page. If you indicate that you will be removing the page after eight seconds, they may try to cram as much information as possible, skewing your test results.

Here's how to perform the eight-second usability test:

1. Ask users to use a search engine that you are fairly confident will show your site in the SERPs.
2. Give them the query to submit.
3. Tell them to look for your company's website in the SERP lists and click it once they find it.
4. Once the resulting page from your site loads, begin to count, silently to yourself, to eight.
5. Close the window after you reach eight seconds.
6. Ask the users
   - Is this the information you expected to see on this page?
   - What page were you on?
   - What words do you recall being on the page? Note any keywords they mention. Compare the keywords the participant mentions with the keywords in your SERP listing.

TIP Eight seconds may seem like an eternity to you, but it will feel very brief to your participants. Give them a full eight seconds. If you are testing on dial-up connection or have download speed considerations, give your users up to 12 seconds. Be consistent—every participant should be given the same amount of time to evaluate a page. Don't make it obvious to the users that you are giving them a specific amount of time, or you may distract them and get skewed data from the test.

Minimally what you are looking for is that users feel the SERP listing brought them to the appropriate page on your site.

FIGURE 9.7 The search engine query that brought users to this page was *surfrider chapters*. In eight seconds, can you tell if this page is the appropriate page for the query *surfrider chapters*? http://surfrider. org/chapters.asp

FIGURE 9.7 The search engine query that brought users to this page was *surfrider chapters*. In eight seconds, can you tell if this page is the appropriate page for the query *surfrider chapters*? http://surfrider. org/chapters.asp

■ OBSERVE NAVIGATIONAL WEB SEARCHES

Watch users perform a navigational search on a commercial search engine. Ask participants to perform a navigational search for your company in their favorite commercial search engine. Be sure there is a good chance of the users finding your site in the intended commercial search engine. This shouldn't be an exercise in futility.

This test may prove especially helpful to companies and organizations whose names use common and/or competitive words and if their company is searchable using abbreviations or multiple name variations.

When you ask the user to perform the search:

- Don't ask them to perform a "navigational search." They probably won't know what that is.

- Don't tell them the name of the company you want them to search for. If you do, they will type exactly what you just asked them to search for.

- Don't tell them the domain of they site you want them to find.

Instead say something like, "Find our company on the Internet using your favorite search engine." A generic statement like this is not leading and leaves it to the users to decide which commercial search engine to use and what words to use to search for your company.

Note how the participants search for your company's website:

- Do they use your proper company name in their query?

- Do they use an abbreviation or an acronym in their query?

- Does your site come back in the SERP across a variety of company name spellings, abbreviations, and so on?

- If they use abbreviations, does your SERP listing use those abbreviations too?

How is your site listed in the SERP? Remember, the users are going to look for their validated query in the SERP.

Try searching for *high point* or *true north* in your favorite search engine. Without a qualifier like *furniture*, *high point* could mean one of hundreds of navigational searches. Similar is true of *true north*.

The search engines may not be able to anticipate all name variations your users might use in their queries. Consider buying your company's name variations via pay-per-click advertising, especially if your company name uses competitive or common words in its name that might make it too difficult to satisfy all user queries with a natural search.

> **NOTE** The longer your company name, the more likely that users will edit, shorten, or abbreviate it in some way when they perform a navigational search.

■ REVIEW SITE SEARCH DATA

Site search queries frequently contain the last words a user searched for before abandoning your website.

By viewing queries in your site search logs, you'll gain an insight into how users are thinking about your content and the keywords users are searching for and not finding on your site.

Your query data will fall into three categories:

- Data that is completely disconnected from the content of your site. Be careful not to misinterpret junk queries as valid queries.

- Valid user queries that your site *doesn't* satisfy.

- Valid user queries that your site *does* satisfy.

It's the last two items that we want to take a closer look at. The second category (valid user queries that your site *doesn't* satisfy) requires you to make some decisions. Just because users are looking for this information doesn't mean you should provide it, if it doesn't complement your business goals. If you decide you want to act on the user site search query, you'll need to decide where to build out the content so your users will be able to find it.

The third category in the list (valid user queries that your site *does* satisfy) suggests that your content is not easily found by primary means of navigation even though it does exist on your website. Users might not be able to find the content because the content is buried too deep in the architecture, or because links to the content are not catching the users' eye, or because navigation labels aren't easy to interpret.

You can improve the findability of this content by conducting usability tests to detect where they lose the scent of information. First, choose a query from your site search data (remember, this data includes the site search queries your site users composed after losing the sent of information). Second, ask your test participants to find the content that best represents the site search query. Note the paths they take to find the content. How do those paths compare with the paths you expected them to take?

Be aware of where your users lose the scent of information on your website. Indications of users losing the scent of information include hesitation in clicking hyperlinks, not knowing what content to expect from clicking hyperlinked copy and graphics, and excessive clicking that results in frustration. Ask your participants to think out loud as they search for content. Participants verbalizing their thoughts and actions will clarify what they are they thinking as they attempt to locate the content.

The report in **Figure 9.8** shows the number of searches and number of relevant results from a WordPress blog. Some queries are more relevant than others. *Hangers*, for example, isn't relevant to the content on the site whatsoever.

FIGURE 9.8 Changes to the site should not be made to accommodate such irrelevant queries such as *hangers*.

Last 30 days		
Term	**Searches**	**Results**
None	5	0
how can going green help bel air high school?	2	0
Mcdonalds French Fries Ingredians	2	0
think green	2	10
bamboo stuff	1	0
bike travel	1	1
Danish	1	0
gas milage	1	1
golf	1	2
hangers	1	0
inflating tires	1	0
thomas mattia	1	1
tires	1	2
tires inflation gas milage	1	0

■ BRAND PERCEPTION TEST

Branding covers a wide range of attributes including graphic elements like logos and corporate fonts. But branding is much more than graphics—it's the emotional connection someone feels for a product or company. Website usability, be it good or bad, affects how users think and feel about your brand.

What first comes to mind when you hear these brand names:

- Apple
- Starbucks
- Google
- McDonald's
- Amazon

You probably have some strong feelings about these brands if you fall into the target market for these companies.

Let's take Apple, for example. Apple's TV campaigns tout its superiority over PC. Apple users probably find the ads smart and funny while a PC user might find the ads arrogant and insulting. Apple is positioning itself as a superior product in a way that resonates with its target market.

The idea behind brand positioning is to get you to think about a product in a way the manufacture wants you to, in order to make an emotional connection with you before you walk into a store, go online, take the car for a test drive, or whatever action you take with a product or service.

Every touch point either enhances or degrades the product positioning and the emotional connection you have with a brand. This also includes websites. Unlike many other touch points, however, you can measure how websites affect branding pretty easily and relatively cheaply by simply asking users about their experience on a website after usability testing.

First, you'll need to get a baseline on the current emotional connection your participants have with your brand and then see if their interaction with the website enhanced their emotional connection, degraded that emotional connection, or didn't move the needle either way.

This can be done formally or informally. If you are trying to get a general feel of how your website is affecting your brand, you can do this verbally with participants. If you're looking to use the results as part of a pitch to get more attention put on your search and web usability initiatives, you should do this more formally and roll up the data into a report with graphs that catch the attention of your management or client.

TIP The ease of finding information and ability to complete a task will affect brand perception. The stronger the scent of information, the stronger your users' emotional connection will be with your website and brand.

What you'll need

- A customer or prospect familiar with your brand.
- Tasks for testing the usability of your website.
- A survey designed to measure branding. We'll look at some sample survey questions in a minute.

What you do

- Before usability testing, give the participants the branding evaluation that asks them how they perceive your brand.
- Perform your choice of usability test(s) with your participants.
- After the usability testing, give the participants the same branding evaluation that asks them how they perceive your brand after taking your usability test.
- Evaluate how/if using your website changes your users' perception of your brand.

Ideally, you want participants to rate your company's brand higher on the post-usability branding evaluation. An increased rating would show that your website is enhancing your brand. Minimally, you want participants to rate your company's brand the same on the pre- and post-usability branding evaluation. If this is the case, take comfort in knowing that your website isn't hurting your brand. Unfortunately, your website isn't helping your branding initiatives either. If you receive lower ratings on your post-usability branding evaluation, you have some work to do on your website.

Be sure the questions you ask are written in a way that the participants know they are evaluating how the website affects their perception of the brand.

For example:

Rate how you feel about COMPANY A before and after interacting with COMPANY A's website.

- Before interacting with COMPANY A's website, I would rate my feelings as

    1) Very Weak 2) Weak 3) Neutral 4) Strong 5) Very Strong

- After interacting with COMPANY A's website, I would rate my feelings as

    1) Very Weak 2) Weak 3) Neutral 4) Strong 5) Very Strong

Some other questions you might want to ask in your branding evaluation, using a similar format as the previous prompts, include

- Rate COMPANY A's trustworthiness before and after interacting with COMPANY A's website.

- Rate COMPANY A's reliability before and after interacting with COMPANY A's website.

- Rate your likelihood of recommending COMPANY A to a friend or family member before and after interacting with COMPANY A's website.

You can add an open-ended question at the end of the second survey to help the users summarize their experience after using your website and get more insight into how they feel about your website, such as, "How would you describe your experience on COMPANY A's website?"

■ CHECK YOUR ERROR MESSAGES

One bad error message may be all that stands between your user and a conversion on your website. Typically error messages come in three flavors:

- Poorly written cryptic techno-language that nobody understands

- Poorly written error messages that were meant to be helpful but aren't

- Well-written error messages that properly explain the error and help users get back on track

Ideally, all of your error messages should fall into that last category.

You might be able to get a document that lists the error messages and the associated page and field(s) that trigger them from your IT group. Chances are, you'll need to go through your site and perform a post-launch QA, creating errors and documenting as you go along.

Your error messages should be so clear and concise that your users can match them up to the field on your web page without having to trigger them by submitting the actual form. One way to confirm if this is true is to bring your error messages in front of users on individual flash cards and ask them to match up the error with the field on the page that would trigger it if the form were submitted. If your users can correctly tell you which field triggers the error message, it's a well-written error message.

For example, the following is part of an error message that the Yahoo Directory delivered because the credit card type didn't match the 16-digit credit card number: *"Invalid Payment Instrument Data"*

Have you ever been asked when checking out at a store, "Is that a debit card or a payment instrument?" Didn't think so.

Here's a proposed error message: *"The credit card type you selected doesn't match the credit card number you entered."*

While you're at it, check your formatting.

Formatting the error message so that the message is physically near with the field causing the error is another form of scent of information. Proper formatting and writing of the error message will greatly reduce users' need to scan and search the page.

■ FREE EXPLORATION TEST

Have you ever watched someone use your website? It seems so obvious, but many of us have never seen someone actually use the websites we help create. Watching a user freely explore your website will open your eyes to stumbling blocks that you may have never considered otherwise.

Have you ever watched someone use your website? It seems so obvious, but many of us have never seen someone actually using our website.

Here's how you conduct a free exploration test:

- Find a participant who matches your site's user profile. Ask if they would be willing to show you how they would use the site to purchase, find, or learn about *X, Y, Z.*

- Tell them you want to see how they would use the site. Ask them to think out loud as they click around.

- Ask them questions when something interesting happens.

Sounds simple enough, right? The idea is to not direct users to do any specific thing. You can direct them later with other tests. For now, let the users self-direct. You're looking to see how they would naturally use the site—as naturally as they would with someone looking over their shoulder asking them questions, that is.

As your participants are going through your site, ask them why they are doing certain things. If they aren't using portions of the navigation, ask them why. You may find out that they didn't even notice the navigation or that the navigation didn't look like navigation to them.

Other items to take note of or ask include

- If they exhibit pogo-sticking behavior (going back forth between pages using one page as an anchor).

- If they quickly scroll down a page scanning for something, ask them what they are looking for.

- Ask them if they know what page they are on after they click through a few pages.

- If they use site search, site map, breadcrumbs, or other forms of secondary navigation, ask them if they normally use those types of navigation. If they do, ask why. If they don't, ask them why they used it on your site.

Showing interest and being curious about your users, without being overbearing, will yield valuable feedback that you can use to improve your website's search usability.

TIP As with any usability test, be clear to your participants that they are not the ones being tested—it's the website that is being tested. Let them know that they are providing valuable feedback that will help make the website better for everyone.

■ DECONSTRUCTING COMMON MYTHS AND MISCONCEPTIONS

Some managers and clients look at search and usability professionals as a means to a quick and permanent solution for a website problem, assuming that one round of SEO changes or one usability test will fix it. They don't understand that what search and usability professionals do is a process that involves constant change based on user feedback.

Following are some common myths dispelled to help you set expectations with your managers and clients and get your search and web usability efforts moving in the right direction.

Myth #1: There Is a Magic Bullet

There is no magic bullet or secret sauce that will solve all your search and web usability problems.

The best any web professional can do to address search and web usability problems is

- Continue to build your toolkit with techniques to better diagnose search and web usability problems appropriately. Is it a navigational, information, or transactional query? Do we need to perform usability testing or not?

- Know when to tap into the individuals who are most appropriate to address the search usability issue of the day. For example, call an information architect if users are getting lost in the website. Call a writer or a graphic designer if a call to action isn't getting users' attention.

- Test your website with your users early and often.

Addressing search and web usability issues can sometimes be a slow, long-term process. Just know that the discoveries you find and the seemingly small changes you make can lead to big gains in your website's search usability.

Myth #2: There's No Such Thing as Perceived vs. Actual Website Speed

A friend of ours went skydiving for the first time last year. As his instructor was giving the details on the jump, he mentioned that the jumpers were going to free-fall for about 45 seconds before the parachute opened.

The instructor replied, "If you're enjoying the free-fall, 45 seconds is not long at all. If you end up hating the free-fall, 45 seconds feels like forever."

Having no prior experience with jumping out of an airplane, our friend asked, "Is 45 seconds a long time to free-fall?"

The instructor replied, "If you're enjoying the free-fall, 45 seconds is not long at all. If you end up hating the free-fall, 45 seconds feels like forever."

Similar is true with perceived website speed and download time. If users are enjoying their time on your site, finding information quickly, accomplishing tasks, they will think your site is fast. If they can't find what they are looking for, or they have trouble completing a task, they will think your site is slow.

Some people find this difficult to believe. Instead of working on perceived download time they work on actual download time. We're not saying to abandon efforts to decrease the actual download time of your site. We absolutely encourage it. Clean up your code, optimize your images, and upgrade your servers. The quicker you can get content to your users the better. But it doesn't stop there. You need to work on perceived download time, too.

Here are some tips to improve perceived download time:

- Help users follow the scent of information from page to page. If your users can find information more easily on your site than your competitors', even if it takes longer, they will feel like they are getting around quickly and will think that you offer a faster site.

- If users can get through a process on your site, such as filling out a form or adding something to cart, with fewer complications and ambiguities, they will have to do less cognitive processing and will think your site is faster than your competitors'.

- Lower user frustration levels and abandonment rates by improving content on help pages and FAQ pages, improving site search results, creating annotated site maps, and providing ambiguity-free error messages.

You still may not believe in perceived download time. Don't take our word for it. Try a little experiment on yourself. Try staring at the wall for one minute. Then watch a one-minute video of your choice on YouTube. Which one felt faster?

Myth #3: The Competition Does It Right

Don't assume that because your competition does something on their website that it's a good idea. Page one SERP listings give the impression that a website is good simply because it has achieved page one results. Often this is not the case.

Blindly keeping up with the Jones' website is no guarantee that it will make your website better.

One company we worked with was determined to have six links in their primary navigation—no more, no less. They came to this conclusion by looking at other industry websites found in the top SERP listings, some of which featured six links in their primary navigation. To them, six was the magic number. They rationalized that by using six primary navigation links they would make their website simple and easy to use.

User testing of the competition's website showed that the six links in the primary navigation buried content, requiring unnecessary clicking, making the desired content difficult or impossible to find. The client's assumptions, based on their own opinions and not on user testing, proved incorrect.

Blindly keeping up with the Jones' website is no guarantee that it will make your website better. Don't assume the way a technique was executed on someone else's website will work for your site. Validate your assumptions with user testing.

Myth #4: You Can Design a "Good" Site Without Feedback from Users

This is a close cousin to "The competition does it right." The difference is instead of assuming that the competition knows your users better than you do, you're assuming that you know your users enough to not talk to them and usability test.

The lack of user-focused and usage-focused design makes people do funny things. People start to assume incorrectly about their users. Those incorrect assumptions equate to wasted money, lost business opportunity, and talented people quitting to go work for someone else.

It's really not that difficult to put together a mediocre site.

The contrary happens when you bring your site in front of users. You will see where you lose users, when they become frustrated, and where they abandon your website. The experience will change your perception of how people get around and use your site.

It's really not that difficult to put together a mediocre site. There are plenty of software applications and tutorials online that will help you technically put together a website. This explains why there are so many mediocre websites. You need to interact with people similar to your users if you want to create a good website.

Myth #5: People Will Use Your Site Since It's the Best of Its Kind

Some people think that if their site is the best in its category, there is no reason to usability test their website. The client's justification: "If you were a user, which site would you use to buy *X?*"

Some site owners have a point. Their website is much better than some of the terrible sites their competition serves up to users. Still, it's risky to assume that your product is so desired that people will do anything, including muddling through a clunky interface, to get it.

Case in point: A friend of ours canceled her trip because the websites she was using to book her airfare were too hard to use and she decided not to go.

It wasn't that she didn't want to go visit her friend; it was that she had other options and she decided, with the help of getting frustrated with a website or two, that she preferred one of the other options instead. Like a road trip that didn't involve finishing an online checkout.

Next time you think, "If I were a user, I would buy from my site because it's the best site out there, albeit still a bad site" think about the hundreds of options users have that might be more desirable than frustratingly muddling through your website not finding the information they want or being unable to finish a task.

Myth #6: You Lose Users After Three Clicks

Most websites are built with a very poor scent of information. As a result, users don't find what they are looking for, get lost, and abandon after three clicks. It doesn't have to be this way.

If you effectively string the scent of information throughout your website, users will keep clicking until they've decided they have gotten what they need. They will decide when to leave because they've found what they were looking for. If their experience was a good one, there's a chance they will be back.

We are led to believe that users abandon after three clicks. It doesn't have to be this way.

Not only will your website see an increased number of returning visitors, but your web analytics will also show you

- Lower bounce rates
- Increased time on site
- Increased page views

WEB ANALYTIC TERMS

Bounce rates—A *bounce* happens when a user leaves your website or a page on your site to go to another website. *Bounce rate* is the percentage of users who leave, or bounce off, your website.

Time on site—As you might have guessed, *time on site* is the amount of time a user spends on your site. It is commonly thought of in terms of average time on site. Time on site can result from either of two reasons: time spent in puzzlement, or time spent in enjoyment. Only usability testing will show you the true reason.

Page views—*Page views* means the number of pages a user views during her or his time on your site. Page views are commonly thought of in terms of average page views per visitor. Page views are not "hits." Many people still think a hit is a page view. A hit is an antiquated web metric and is not the same as a page view.

What's even better: These happy users will tell others about your site via links pointing to your site from websites and blogs, social networking sites like Facebook, and social bookmarking sites like del.icio.us.

To sum it up, a good scent of information equals happy users, which results in more quality inbound links and, as a result, better search engine rankings.

Myth #7: The User Is the Problem

We can't tell you how many times we've heard from website builders regarding how users get around their site and that they are doing it wrong. Essentially, what they are saying is that the user, not the website, is the problem.

Contrary to what some people think, the user isn't the problem. The problem is the website, and it should be changed.

That sentiment is often expressed in one of the following fashions by website owners, developers, designers, and others working on the site:

"They [users] should do it this way."

"I would do it this way."

"This is the best way to do it."

Contrary to what some people think, the user isn't the problem. The problem is the website, and it should be changed. You can be apathetic and ignore your users until they go away, or you can be empathetic and help your users, and they will eventually make your site a success.

Myth #8: The User Is Always Right

Just because the user isn't the problem doesn't mean the user is always right.

A tomato is never going to be a vegetable no matter how many users wanted to find tomatoes under vegetables.

Case in point: In a usability test, when asked to locate the tomato page of a fruits and vegetables website, 60 percent of users initially went to the vegetable section. About 33 percent of those who did not find the tomato page under vegetables looked for tomatoes under fruits.

A tomato is never going to be a vegetable no matter how many users wanted to find tomatoes under vegetables.

You may find that users look for information on your site in an area that obviously shouldn't house the information, like a tomato page under the vegetable category. One way to remedy this type of situation is to list a blurb on a page about tomatoes under vegetables. Something to the effect of:

<u>Tomato</u> *You can find more information on tomatoes under fruits.*

(The above link takes users to the tomato page under fruits.)

By taking into account the high percentage of users who think a tomato is a vegetable, we are educating and helping users find their content without changing the definition of a tomato, without creating duplicate content, and without losing users who know that a tomato is a fruit.

Myth #9: Usability Tests Are 100% Accurate

Usability tests arguably produce the best type of feedback you can get. They are a one-to-one, in-person, direct method of research that gives the administrator a chance to ask follow-up questions to clear up any questions he or she might have from the test session.

So why are usability tests not 100 percent accurate?

Test subjects, just like students in school, know they are being tested. As a result, they tend to try a little harder than they would in their natural environment at home or work.

> *No natural environment, be it work or home, is 100 percent distraction free of kids, spouses, colleagues, phones, instant messaging, texting, or pets.*

Most people will abandon the task much sooner in their natural environment than your test subjects in a testing environment. Additionally, the testing environment is usually designed to be distraction free. No natural environment, be it work or home, is 100 percent distraction free of kids, spouses, colleagues, phones, instant messaging, texting, or pets.

TIP Increase your usability testing accuracy by testing the appropriate number of test participants. You'll know you are finished testing when you start hearing test participants say the same thing. For most tests 5–10 users per group will be sufficient.

Myth #10: Users Will Figure Out What Is a Link by Clicking It

Just because you aren't putting white links on a white background doesn't mean you aren't hiding links from users. By not making clickable items look obviously clickable (affordance) you are obscuring their function and the scent of information along with it.

> *Don't force users to read your mind. If something is clickable, make it look clickable. If something is not clickable, don't make it look clickable.*

Users decide what is clickable before they move their mouse, not when their mouse happens to rollover a page element and the arrow becomes a hand.

Don't force users to read your mind. If something is clickable, make it look clickable. If something is not clickable, don't make it look clickable. This philosophy of making things represent their functionality should be carried across all page elements.

The more you make users think about how your site functions, the quicker they will tire and you will lose them.

Myth #11: Usability Guidelines Will Make Your Site Successful

TIP *The Design of Sites* by Douglas K. van Duyne, James A. Landay, and Jason I. Hong is a good place to review web usability guidelines.

Not every usability guideline is applicable or will work for your site as each website and task flow is unique. You must usability test to see what works for your site and your task flow. Only then will you understand why users respond the way they do to your website.

A colleague of ours did all the "right things" to her shopping cart with the intention of improving her conversion rate. Unfortunately, she didn't usability test her changes. Her first round of feedback on the changes came from live users who abandoned her shopping cart at a rate of 2.5 times that of her original design.

Without fully understanding the reasons why all the "right things" didn't work she reverted back to the previous design.

Following web usability guidelines is a good place to start, but they are only one tool in the search usability toolbox. Nothing beats testing your own site.

Myth #12: The Web Is Yours

David Weinberger, author, philosopher, and marketer, sums up companies' view of the web like this: "… [T]he big mistake businesses make isn't the economic or technical. It's the psychological or (dare I say?) spiritual. They're not getting the biggest 'it' there is to get: The web isn't theirs. The web is ours." (From the essay "Explaining the Passion that Powers the Web," published in *Best Practice: Ideas and Insights from the World's Foremost Business Thinkers*.)

What Weinberger is saying is that while it may be your website, it's the users' experience you need to design for. If not, your website and possibly your business will fail.

■ CONCLUSION

Here are the key points of this chapter:

- Using the reverse card sort test to add well-organized structure to an existing site will increase your search visibility and make it easier for users to find the content they are looking for.

- To meet users' expectations and reduce abandons, ask users what content or functionality they would expect from clicking every link on your home page.

- Watching users perform a navigational search on a commercial search engine will show you how/if users locate your site in the SERPs.

- Users turning to site search results can show symptoms of your website's lack of scent of information.

- Bad error messages can make or break conversions. Check to see if yours are written in a language your users will understand.

- There is no magic bullet. There is no secret sauce. It's a lot of hard work to improve your website's search and web usability.

- Perceived download time is just as important, and maybe more so, than actual download time.

- Just because the competition does something on their site doesn't mean you should do it on your site.

- If you want to design a good website that meets users' goals and business objectives, you must talk to your users.

- Keep the scent of information strong and people will follow it further than three clicks deep.

- Users typically aren't the problem when they can't find information; more likely, your site needs to be changed.

- Conduct usability testing if you want to know how easy it is for users to find information on your website.

- If something is clickable, make it look clickable. If it isn't clickable, don't make it look clickable.

- Blindly following usability guidelines won't make your site successful. Combining usability guideline with user testing will.

- It may be your website, but it's your users' experience. Treat your users with respect and they will treat you well.

■ INDEX

Symbol

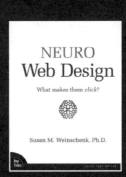

Search Engine Visibility
Second Edition

"Search Engine Visibility is the best introduction to SEO on the market. It breaks down the walls between engineering, marketing, and design by illustrating how structure, content, and code can work together to deliver optimal findability and a better user experience."

> **PETER MORVILLE**, Author of *Ambient Findability: What We Find Changes Who We Become*

Search Engine Visibility is a must-read for Web designers and developers, search engine optimizers, usability professionals, and marketers who are seeking to create more effective Web sites that meet both user and business goals. Besides outlining ways to obtain top positions in search results, this book shows you how to design, write, and create user-friendly Web sites. This new edition of Search Engine Visibility includes up-to-date coverage of blogs, podcasts (both video and audio), Web applications, and more. It also shows you pitfalls to avoid.

Search Engine Visibility, Second Edition
Shari Thurow
ISBN: 9780321503244
312 Pages

Topics covered in this book include:

• How to write search engine friendly sales copy

• Search engine friendly design solutions

• Ways to increase your Web site's popularity

• Solutions for dynamic Web sites